THE LANGUAGE DEVELOPMENT OF THE PRESCHOOL CHILD

UNIVERSITY OF MINNESOTA
THE INSTITUTE OF CHILD WELFARE
MONOGRAPH SERIES NO. IV

THE LANGUAGE DEVELOPMENT
OF THE PRESCHOOL CHILD

By

DOROTHEA A. McCARTHY, PH.D.

INSTITUTE OF CHILD WELFARE
UNIVERSITY OF MINNESOTA

GREENWOOD PRESS, PUBLISHERS
WESTPORT, CONNECTICUT

Library of Congress Cataloging in Publication Data

McCarthy, Dorothea Agnes, 1906-1974.
  The language development of the preschool child.

    Reprint of the ed. published by the University of
  Minnesota Press, Minneapolis, which was issued as no. 4.
  of Monograph series of the Institute of Child Welfare,
  University of Minnesota.
    Originally presented as the author's thesis, Univer-
  sity of Minnesota, 1929.
    Bibliography: p.
    Includes index.
    1. Children--Language. 2. Child study. I. Title.
  II. Series. Minnesota. University. Institute of Child
  Development and Welfare. Monograph series ; no. 4.
  LB1139.L3M3 1975   372.6'01'9   74-141549
  ISBN 0-8371-5896-6

Originally published in 1930 by the University of Minnesota
Press, Minneapolis

Reprinted with the permission of the University of Minnesota
Press

Reprinted in 1975 by Greenwood Press, Inc.,
51 Riverside Avenue, Westport, Conn. 06880

Library of Congress catalog card number 74-141549
ISBN 0-8371-5896-6

Printed in the United States of America

10 9 8 7 6 5 4 3

FOREWORD

Previous studies of the development of language in early childhood, have, as a rule, been concerned with one or two children or with selected groups. In the study that is here presented, Dr. McCarthy has taken unusual precautions to secure a group representative of the general population by selecting her children within each age level on the basis of socio-economic status. Further control has been secured by obtaining an equal number of responses for each child, by limiting the age groups to children within a month of the age specified, and by equating the number of individuals in each age and sex group.

The analysis of the data is unusually complete. In addition to a study of the length and structure of the sentence and of the use of parts of speech, an interesting modification of the Piaget functional analysis has been used. The relationship of various language processes to age, sex, socio-economic status, intelligence, position in family, number of playmates, and other factors has been investigated.

On the basis of the number of controls utilized in selecting the subjects and the care and thoroughness with which the data are analyzed, this monograph stands out as one of the best studies of the development of language which has yet appeared. It is, I think, an excellent example of the scientific possibilities inherent in the study of child development.

JOHN E. ANDERSON
Director, Institute of Child Welfare

ACKNOWLEDGMENTS

It gives me great pleasure to express my appreciation and gratitude to Dr. Florence L. Goodenough and to Dr. John E. Anderson, of the Institute of Child Welfare of the University of Minnesota, whose unfailing interest, helpful suggestions, and criticisms were of inestimable value in the preparation of this monograph.

Many thanks are due to all those through whose coopera- tion the subjects of this study were obtained; particularly, Miss Helen Peck, Miss Hazel Frasch, Mrs. Genevieve Carlson, and Miss Mary Isabelle Rochette of the Infant Welfare Society of Minneapolis; as well as the directors of the day nurseries at Northeast Neighborhood House, Pillsbury House, Wells Memorial House, Unity House, and the Margaret Barry House, and the superintendents of the Stevens Avenue Home, the Lutheran Children's Friend Society, the Salvation Army Home; and also, the many mothers of preschool children of Minne- apolis through whose gracious cooperation this study was made possible.

I take this opportunity to thank Miss Marion L. Mattson, Miss Mildred Parten, and Mrs. Emily Payetta Turney, who gave willingly of their time to score for reliability.

Finally, I express my gratitude to my parents, Francis D. McCarthy and Mary Molloy McCarthy for their interest, encouragement, and assistance during the course of this investigation.

DOROTHEA A. MCCARTHY

University of Minnesota
September, 1929.

CONTENTS

LIST OF TABLES

LIST OF FIGURES

CHAPTER I

PREVIOUS INVESTIGATIONS IN THE FIELD

INTRODUCTION

Language is a term that is applied to a system of symbolic habits which each individual learns so early in life that he cannot remember the process of its acquisition. Definitions of language vary to such an extent that one hesitates to use the term because of the very broad, and the very narrow, interpretations that it may receive. For some it includes all forms of expression; not only verbal expression, but expression in the form of gestures, music, art, and sculpture. Hence, the term is really much broader than the term "speech," which is often used synonomously with it. The definitions of the grammarians represent the opposite extreme, in which language is limited to that form of verbal expression which conforms to the conventional rules of grammar.

As used in this presentation, the term "language" has neither of these extreme meanings. It is used to mean vocal expression to the exclusion of other forms of expression, and yet it is ·much more inclusive than the grammarians allow. As Preyer [58] says, true language occurs when the child first uses a word of verbal language or the nurse's jargon independently and correctly. Stern [63] says that language begins when "the child first utters a sound with full .consciousness of its meaning and for the purpose of communication." According to such criteria, conformity to the complex rules of grammar should not determine whether or not a response is to be included as language. In the present investigation, therefore, we will consider the ontogenesis of vocal responses and their integration into the verbal language or speech of the adult.

1

Language is generally admitted to be the most outstanding feature that distinguishes man from the lower animals. When we consider the tremendous gap between man and the lower animals in intellectual development, we realize to some extent the vast importance of language for the race, and the invaluable inheritance every normal child has in the mother tongue. Consider also, how little beyond the animal level a deaf child is able to progress without a great deal of painstaking instruction in the use of other avenues of sense.

Another fact that brings out the important rôle of language is the meager communication and corresponding dearth of culture and civilization among primitive peoples. The greatest contrast in intellectual development between them and the civilized world is essentially a matter of language. And this brings us to a consideration of the widespread use of language in its various forms, oral and written, in the civilization of today. We engage in few activities in which language is not intimately involved. It is such an integral part of our whole reaction system that it is automatic, and we seldom stop to think how constantly we use overt language. MacDougall [39] says:

The beginning of speech is the most momentous event in the history of the child. Its understanding is a key to the whole storehouse of knowledge, and upon its use all human fellowship depends. As the means of social intercourse, the repository of learning, and the general instrument of intelligence, the invention of language constitutes the greatest single achievement of human evolution.

In a practical way we are reminded of the frequent necessity for the use of language when we travel in foreign countries. The inability to communicate with those around us becomes most annoying, and when forced to use the minimum of language, we use it only for the things we really need and want. In such situations people revert to the primitive and natural gesture language that is universally

understood. If one tries to acquire a foreign language late
in life, the difficulties involved for the adult in the learning
process make one marvel at the ease and rapidity with which
the little child, so early in his intellectual development, learns
the mother tongue. It is, indeed, one of the most fascinating
and elusive problems of genetic psychology and one of such
vital importance to so many theoretical and practical problems, that the psychologist cannot afford to neglect such a
fertile field of investigation. To mention some of the questions
upon which language has a direct bearing, we may consider
the old proposition that Watson has rediscovered for us in his
article entitled *The Unverbalized in Human Behavior* [74]—that
memory depends on verbalization, or language habits, associated with a situation. As evidence we have the fact that an
individual's memory probably does not extend beyond the
time when he began to talk and to verbalize about events that
he experienced. In the second place, we have the controversial
problem that the behaviorists have revived for us—that of the
identity of thought and language. Whether or not there is
thought without words is a problem which worried the
philosophers long ago, and which is still a puzzle. Some of
the arguments in this controversy will be presented in
Chapter VII.

In spite of the tremendous theoretical and practical
importance of language, it is surprising how little attention
has been paid to it by psychologists. One may pick up any
number of general texts on psychology in which the topic of
language does not appear in the index, or, if it does, it is often
dismissed very summarily in a sentence or at most a paragraph.
Interest in language has been exhibited chiefly in the form of
speculations by philosophers and philologists, all of which
are of very little value to the scientific psychologist. They
may give him hints as to hypotheses that may be tested out
experimentally, but in themselves these speculations contribute

nothing to our body of knowledge about language and its development. The earliest record we have of an experimental approach to the origin of language, and probably the earliest experiment on infants, was that of the Egyptian king, Psammeticus, who died in 610 B. C. He is reported by Chamberlain [12] and many other writers to have ordered two children isolated and brought up by a shepherd who was not to speak either to them or in their presence. The first word they uttered was *bekos,* which means bread in the Phrygian language. From this, the king concluded that Phrygian was the original language of man. While of course the conclusion is naïve, this really constituted the first attempt at an experimental approach to the problem, and we still find that it is to children that we must turn in investigating language development.

Philologists have gone far with their science, which deals with an aspect of language rather far removed from the present problems. Anatomists and physiologists have described the structure and function of the larynx and of all the organs involved in the production of vocal sounds. Phoneticists have analyzed these sounds, and the philosophers have contributed their bit of speculation, and yet our knowledge of the complex habits of speech and of the process of their acquisition is very meager. The psychologist's contribution is almost nil. What work has been done, however, has been almost entirely on children. Interest in the problem was greatest at the time of the child study movement in the last decades of the nineteenth century. Nearly every psychologist recorded detailed observations on his children, and incidentally the children's speech came in for its share of recording. Some of these observations were carried out with a definite interest in the language development of the young child; for example, those by Gale [23]; Gale and Gale [24,25]; Bateman [2,3,4,5]; Brandenburg [8]; Brandenburg and Brandenburg [9,10]; and many others. Most of the early studies that we find reported in the literature are, however, of this biographical nature, and many of them are merely anecdotal accounts of the general development of individual children. Each one is recorded differently, the observations are made under different conditions, and most of them are subject to the unreliability of parents' reports. Hence, very little material that may be considered of scientific value has been contributed by these studies.

The earliest study of this sort of which we have any record is that by Tiedemann, which was done in Germany in 1787. This study has recently been translated into English by Murchison and Langer,[47] who said that this study is "usually regarded as the first attempt to make a series of scientific observations of the behavior of young children." The observations here recorded are done with great care, and aside from the subjectivity of some of the interpretations, are essentially the same sort of things that we are recording in our infant studies of today. This investigation, and the long line of similar observations that have succeeded it, consist mainly of the diary type of anecdote, which merely states that on a particular date, in certain circumstances, child X showed this new accomplishment. While such material is stimulating and suggestive, what can be done with it in and of itself? The conditions are not kept the same for the various children on which these reports are made, the single factor under consideration has not been isolated, and the methods of recording are different in every case. How then can one determine any scientific conclusions from these series of isolated facts? We can simply note the tendency for the most conspicuous traits to appear at approximately the same times. The material is in the state of a collection of baby books, in each of which different aspects of the child's development were observed.

The anatomical mechanism with which the oral sounds of language are made is well described by Allport.[1] He gives excellent plates illustrating the anatomy of the larynx and associated structures and gives a very good account of the neurological processes involved. He explains the beginning of language in the individual; that is, the association of the sound with the object or action, by the conditioned reflex principle. The first utterance of the child, which is mentioned by nearly all writers, is the birth cry, which receives all sorts of interpretations, from the mere reflex gasp for the first breath to an expression of joy, or perhaps of sorrow, at entrance into the world.

DEVELOPMENTAL STAGES

THE BABBLING STAGE

The next step in the prelinguistic stages of the child is the babbling stage, which consists of a variety of sounds uttered at random in a sort of vocal play. Nearly all of the writers who begin their observations on the young infant record in their own phonetic notations, which are very puzzling to decipher, the exact nature of these first utterances. The general agreement seems to be that the vowels appear first, particularly the various "a" sounds are recorded most frequently. The consonants appear later according to most writers, but there seems to be a great deal of variation of opinion as to the order of their appearance. O'Shea [53] traces these prelinguistic stages, which he says include the first eight months, as follows: The early vocal expression is reflex, and for the first two weeks is an undifferentiated squall probably expressive of some sort of discomfort. Between the second and fifth weeks, he reports, the primitive squall begins to be differentiated to denote special forms of discomfort, and from this point differentiation progresses rapidly so that soon all the child's vital experiences may be revealed in specialized ways.' The infant's vocal register, he says, is at the outset limited to sounds indicated in a general way by "a" or "ua." He goes up and down the vowel register for some time before he can execute consonant sounds. The first of these to appear may be denoted generally by "m," "p," and "b." The labials are probably the first executed, then follow in order the gutturals, dentals, and finally the nasals.

The opinions as to the make-up of this babbling vocabulary seem to vary considerably, for Hinckley [31] says, "Preyer thinks that all sounds necessary for future language are now produced, whereas Ament thinks the number of possible sounds is infinite and that it is only with difficulty that the child sinks from this wealth of sounds to the meager level of his mother tongue." Probably, in the young infant, very few articulate or at least distinguishable sounds appear, but certainly in the infant who has had time in which to practice his vocal play, we find many sounds for which we have no written symbols, sounds which have so completely disappeared from the verbal repertoire of the adult that he is unable to imitate them. Hence, it is probable that the diversity of opinion on this point is due to the difference in the ages of the children who were observed.

Taine [66] comments as follows on this early period, "There is the same spontaneous apprenticeship for cries as for movements. The progress of the vocal organ goes on just like that of the limbs; the child learns to emit such or such a sound as it learns to turn its head or its eyes, that is to say, by gropings and constant attempts." In the record of his child he says that only vowels were used up to three and one-half months. "By degrees consonants were added to the vowels and the exclamations became more and more articulate. It all ended in a very distinct twittering."

Major [41] says that "the babbling process or period has all the appearance of getting together a mass of raw material which is to be put into intelligible and significant forms later when the building proper begins," or, as Sully is reported by

Major [41] to have said, "The speech protoplasm begins to differentiate and to assume definite forms." The same author says that this babbling stage lasts until about the second half of the first year or the first quarter of the second year.

Some writers maintain that speech is instinctive, not that the particular language which an individual finally learns to speak is instinctive, but rather that it is instinctive for every normal infant to exercise the muscles involved in the production of speech, just as the random movements of the gross muscles of the body also appear naturally and, as some would say, instinctively. Kirkpatrick [35] says that the fundamental factor involved here is the "tendency to respond by movement of some kind to every stimulus received."

IMITATION

Following this period of babbling and voice play most writers report a tendency to imitation that appears in all functions, but which is most marked in a tendency to imitate the sounds made by other people. According to Conradi,[14] Franke believes that creation without imitation in the development of child language is very rare. Champneys [13] reports the following regarding the observations that he made: "From nine months the child distinctly imitated the intonation of the voice when any word or sentence was repeated in the same way several times." Darwin [15] also mentions this factor of imitation, for he says, "At this date (113th day) I thought . . . . that he began to try to imitate sounds, as he certainly did at a considerably later period." Grant [28] quotes Preyer as follows: " 'It [imitation] is without doubt the first and most important factor in the learning of language, by the individual.' " Stern [63] in his section on imitation in speech says:

The child learning to talk, is no more a mere repetition machine than he is an absolute creator of speech; but his speech-development is

only effected by the combined action of imitation and spontaneity.
. . . . The child can, of course, only become familiar with this mother-
tongue, at first so strange to his ears, by continually hearing it, and only
make it his own by repeating its sounds; thus imitation is, in truth, the
factor which, above all others, makes it possible to learn to speak.

O'Shea [53] maintains that the child's first verbal imitations
are concerned primarily with the motor processes to make
words. In speaking of the seventeenth and eighteenth months,
Pollock [57] says, "The vocabulary is now increasing fast, and
almost any word proposed to the child is imitated with some
real effort at correctness." Whipple and Whipple [75] report
that in their child, imitation became very active at about nine
months of age. In the observations of Tiedemann,[47] mentioned above, he says, "The impulse to imitation develops very
early and seems to have its original source in an instinct."
Thus it seems from these many indications in the literature,
that the factor of imitation plays an important part in the
learning of language. We know also that the language that
a child hears spoken by those about him is the language that
he acquires. Imitation, of course, is a question upon which
there has been a great deal of controversy in psychological
circles. Some of the different points of view as to what is
meant by imitation and its rôle in the learning process will
be presented in Chapter VII.

The First Word

Simultaneously with, or following very closely upon, this
imitative stage we find reported the occurrence of the first
word. This is the measure of the child's linguistic development that is probably most affected by the subjectivity of the
parents' report. When the child first uses a sound with meaning
is very difficult to determine. The first words reported are
frequently what we would call baby words, that is, not real
words of accepted language, but rather certain utterances
which happened to occur simultaneously with certain situations

or events, and which the fond parents interpreted as having meaning in the situation.

Bateman [4] has written a paper on this topic of the first word, in which he tabulates its occurrence as reported in the literature prior to 1917. The list includes eighteen English-speaking children, twelve German-speaking children, and five of various other nationalities. The most frequent occurrence of the first word from these data was at ten months of age. He reports that 74.28 per cent of the children have begun articulate speech by the end of the first year. O'Shea [53] says that conventional words are not usually employed before the completion of the first year. The child spontaneously makes combinations and gives them meaning by attaching them to particular experiences. He further remarks that the child at this time uses words which at first were spontaneous, but which the people around him have conventionalized.

These first words are usually monosyllables, or if they are dissyllables, they usually consist of reduplications, as "mamma," "dada," "papa," "bebe," and the like. Perez [55] reports that for a long time they rebel against real dissyllables, and that the roots or first attempts are monosyllabic sounds. They more easily pronounce reduplicated monosyllables.

THE SINGLE-WORD SENTENCE

Usually we think of the word as the unit of speech, and that after a few words are acquired they are combined into sentences which express complete thoughts; for, according to the grammatical definition, a sentence is a group of words that expresses a complete thought. We can hardly say, however, that the young child does not express a complete thought until he first uses a sentence which is structurally complete. Certainly he expresses his wishes, needs, and attitudes in a most expressive gesture language long before any true language has appeared, and this very effective gesture language persists throughout the period of the acquisition of speech and greatly facilitates the child's expression. Moreover, when we consider only the vocal expression, we must admit that the child expresses, by inflection at least, complete thoughts long before the appearance of the first true sentence.

We find a great deal of evidence to this effect in the literature as indicated by such phrases as the "sentence-word" and the "single-word sentence." Miss Sullivan, in one of her letters about Helen Keller [34] says, "Like her baby cousin, she expresses whole sentences by single words. 'Milk' with a gesture means, 'Give me more milk,' etc. . . . . but the whole sentence repeated many times during the day must in time impress itself upon the brain, and by and by she will use it herself." Lukens [38] makes similar statements: "It is well known that children, in the latter part of the first year and the first part of the second year, often use single words to express their thoughts." And again he states, "Such words are undifferentiated sentence-words, and are similar to such exclamations as 'Fire!' or 'Thief!' There is no grammar to such expressions, since grammar has to do with the relation of different words to each other, and here there is only one word." Pelsma [54] also comments, "The first expressions of the child should be called sentence-words rather than 'parts of speech.' It is the whole of speech. When E. cried 'ma' it was a complete thought expressed." The same author quotes Herbert Spencer, who said, " 'Language was made before grammar.' " Sully's [64] remark regarding this point is, "As with the race, so with the child, the sentence precedes the word. Moreover, each of the child's so-called words in his single-worded talk stands for a considerable variety of sentence forms." Guillaume [29] expresses the same point of view when he states, "Ils (les premiers mots) étaient d'abord compris et prononcés isoléments commes mots-phrases." Wundt [76] says, "Indeed, the sentence appears first as a single whole and is later broken up into its components." Koffka,[37] too, speaks of "words spoken as one-word sentences with a wish or affective character." So we see from these statements that the same word "mamma" may mean "Mamma give me," "Mamma come here," or "Mamma look," according to the inflection with which it is uttered. Many of the early sounds can be clearly recognized as imperative in tone or perhaps exclamatory in function, and the questioning inflection is quite unmistakable even in the monosyllabic utterances. It is on the basis of such findings as these, that the classifications used in the present investigation are based, as will be brought out in the next chapter.

SENTENCE FORMATION

Following the acquisition of the first word and the rapid increase in the vocabulary, we find the child beginning to combine words. The first combination is usually the noun-verb combination, and thereafter there is a rapid development of the sentence. Few of the writers on children's language have indicated any interest in this aspect of linguistic development, which really is of great importance, for what does it matter how many single words the child knows if he cannot use them and combine them into sentences in order adequately to express his thoughts? Aside from the incidental anecdotes on the first sentence, practically the only attempts to study sentence formation have been those by Nice [50] and Smith.[61] The various stages of sentence formation as traced by Nice [50] are as follows:

1. *The single-word stage*, from four to nine months for eighteen English speaking children.

2. *The early sentence stage.*—The first sentence appears between thirteen and twenty-seven months for English speaking children, with an average at seventeen and one-half months. A large percentage of these sentences are incomplete. The vocabulary at this time ranges from 14 to 180 words, and there

is what she calls a "baby ratio" of 65 per cent or more of nouns. The usual duration of this stage is from four to seven months.

3. *The short sentence stage*, in which the child has not mastered inflections and is omitting many minor words. In this stage the sentences are from 3.5 to 4.5 words. The mean is never as low as 3 or as high as 5 words. At this time she reports that only one or two sentences out of fifty are compound or complex. The child frequently omits auxiliaries, articles, pronouns, prepositions, and conjunctions. The range of vocabularies at this time is from 475 to 1,135 words, with a "stable ratio" of nouns, 50 to 60 per cent, and verbs, 20 to 24 per cent. This information is based on the records of only three cases. There is a very short transition stage going over very quickly into the next type of sentence.

4. *The complete sentence stage* (sentences of six to eight words), which appears after four years. All normal children, she says, show approximately the same length of sentence at this stage. By this time the inflections have been practically mastered, and the majority of the sentences are complete. The vocabulary of the complete sentence stage is estimated at about one thousand words. The same stages are traced for the French- and German-speaking children.

Smith [61] has recorded the spontaneous conversation of eighty-eight children from two to five years of age. Her results on the mean length of sentence are given in Chapter III for comparison with those of the present investigation. She says regarding her sentence analysis,

The most significant trend in the development of the sentence with increase of age was an increasing tendency toward the use of longer and more complete sentences. . . . . Declarative sentences predominated at all ages. . . . . Other trends that may be significant were a decrease with age in the proportion of simple sentences to complex and compound sentences, an increase in the number of questions, and a decrease with age in exclamatory sentences.

VOCABULARIES

METHODS OF COUNTING

It is from the time of the appearance of these first words that the various vocabulary counts, which list the words in the order of their appearance, begin and continue for various lengths of time, some of them until five years of age. The methods used by the different investigators are all very different, so that an adequate comparison of their results is practically an impossibility, unless one were to use the most rigid rules of counting that were used by any of the investigators and recount and reclassify all the vocabularies that are published in full. Doran [20] has published in condensed form all the statistics published before 1907 on the vocabularies of children below school age, simply as they were published, regardless of the method used in recording, or of the method of counting. His table includes ninety-eight vocabularies of children ranging in age from eight to seventy-two months. Some of the records, however, represent vocabularies of the same children at different ages.

Some investigators, particularly the Gales,[25] Nice,[49] and the Brandenburgs,[10] have used the all-day conversation method of recording children's speech. From such a record, of course, more than a vocabulary count can be obtained, since it could yield valuable material on sentence length and structure. Few of the writers who have recorded their data in such form have evinced an interest in sentence formation. Nice [50] has indicated a greater interest in this aspect than most of the other writers and has given some very stimulating indications. Many other writers, especially Bateman,[3] have recorded their material in the form of conversation but have not taken the whole conversation for any one day.

The writers who are interested chiefly in vocabulary counts, however, record simply the different words used. Some record them in the order of their acquisition (Boyd [7]). Deville [17] recorded the words acquired each month from the twentieth to the twenty-fourth months, inclusive. The Whipples,[75] Bateman,[5] and others engaged the child in conversation in order to elicit all the words that the child was able to use, even though they did not occur in his spontaneous conversation. Beyer [6] included words used spontaneously and apparently understood by the child. He omitted all words that the child had used previous to the two months' period of observation, as well as those which occurred in the early part of the observation, and which were apparently forgotten during the course of the investigation. Certainly the results so obtained could hardly be comparable with the results obtained by the method of eliciting words in conversation, and by using a dictionary, and other published vocabularies of children, in efforts to secure all the words that the child knows.

Another error enters such studies when they are continued over a long period of time. The child's language is developing very rapidly at these early ages, and his vocabulary is constantly changing, chiefly in the direction of increase in the number of words known, but also by the dropping out of some of the early words. There seems to be agreement among the writers on the subject that words that occur in songs, poems, and nursery rhymes, which are learned parrot-fashion, and which probably are not understood by the child, should not be included in the lists of words. A point, however, on which they disagree very frequently is the question of whether or not the inflections of verbs, adjectives, and pronouns should be counted as different words. The most usual point of view on this matter is that which Bateman [5] has adopted, namely, to include the variants as different words if they are from different roots; that is, if there is a fundamental change in the word, as in most irregular verbs and adjectives. These rules have been used by Nice [51] and practically the same policy was adopted by Drever.[21] In view of these facts, this is the method that has been adopted in the word analysis of the present investigation. Brandenburg [8] published his results both with and without the variants included. The Whipples [75] say:

Contrary to the custom of some writers, we have included inflected endings (except plurals), grammatical variants and compounds. . . . . It seems unnecessary to point out.that psychologically speaking, related forms like these are just as much distinct acquisitions for the child as are totally different words: . . . . the principles of exclusion that have been adopted by some compilers of children's vocabularies, notably by Holden, may be grammatically, but they are not psychologically justifiable.

PARTS OF SPEECH IN VOCABULARIES

Practically all these vocabularies are reported in classifications according to the various parts of speech. Most of the reports give the actual number of nouns, of verbs, etc., and when the total number of words in the vocabularies differs so markedly, the comparisons are very difficult to make without converting them into percentages. Tabulation according to percentages enables one to note the relationships of the various parts of speech within an age group, and from age to age, more readily. The most obvious fact that comes out of the classifications according to the parts of speech is the preponderance of nouns in the younger age groups. Most of the reports give 50 or 60 per cent nouns at the two-year level. Grant,[28] who has made an extensive survey of the published vocabularies, states that "by referring to the comparative table of vocabularies, it will be seen that most vocabularies are made up of even more than 50 per cent nouns. In general, the proportion of nouns to the entire vocabulary decreases as the vocabulary increases, and the proportion of verbs increases accordingly."

This is interesting in view of the fact that it is coincident with what most writers call the naming stage of language development. The first word is usually the name of an object or of a person, and hence is what we term a noun. Koffka [37] remarks in connection with this stage of development, "The name question seems to be the important factor and the one upon which progress is chiefly based. . . . . The most important discovery in the child's life is the discovery that everything has a name."

The importance of this discovery is clearly brought out by Helen Keller [34] in her autobiography when she says, regarding her discovery that the letters "w-a-t-e-r" in the manual alphabet represented the name for the cool stream that gushed over her hand: "Somehow the mystery of language was revealed to me. I knew then that "w-a-t-e-r" meant the wonderful cool something that was flowing over my hand. . . . . I left the well-house eager to learn. Everything had a name, and each new name gave birth to a new thought."

Moore [46] mentions that at nineteen and one-half months her child had the habit of naming each thing and that all the words of the first year were proper nouns. She says that next a few common nouns were added from the fifty-second to the eighty-second week, and that after the eighty-second week, the acquisition of nouns proceeded rapidly. This is typical of most of the reports of the vocabularies of these early stages.

Interjections are also found to form quite a large proportion of the words of the younger children, especially when we consider the small number of them in the language. Moore [46] reports that they are among the earliest words in the vocabulary and, in fact, they are so noticeable in the child's vocabulary that many writers have postulated the interjectional theory of the origin of language.

There are several factors that enter into these reports on the parts of speech, however, that tend to indicate that the large percentage of nouns may be an artifact resulting from the

method of recording, or some such source. The first consideration in this regard has to do with the above-mentioned factor
of the one-word sentence. It is true that the one-word sentence often consists of the name of a person or object, and
.hence we class it as a noun. But, as was brought out before,
and as is recognized by so many writers, this one word has
the function of a whole sentence. Lukens [38] points out the
difficulty involved here very clearly when he states:

> To classify such child-words by the adult distinctions of the parts of
> speech . . . . is of course to be misled by very superficial considera-
> tions. It does not seem possible to classify a child's words until he uses
> all of the parts of speech; unless indeed we were to follow Dewey in
> speaking of them as "nominal-adjectival-verbal," etc.

Sully [64] also remarks about this same point, "We must not
suppose that the words used in this simple disjointed talk have
their full grammatical value." And the Whipples [75] state that
"the child in many ways does psychological violence to the
technical classifications of grammar." So we see that these
words, which the dictionary lists as nouns, really function not
only as nouns, but as verbs, adjectives, interjections, and almost
any part of speech that is needed in the situation. Dewey [19]
emphasizes the fact that

> The psychological classification is to class the word according to what
> it means to a child, not to the adult with his grammatical forms all
> differentiated. . . . . Such classification would in all probability in-
> crease immensely the percentage of verbs. It is true that such a method
> demands more care in observation, and opens the way to the very
> variable error of interpretation; but the greater certainty of the method
> followed above is after all only seeming—it does not express the *child's*
> vocabulary, but our interpretation of it according to a fixed but highly
> conventional standard. . . . . What I would suggest, then, along the
> line of a study of the distribution of vocabulary into parts of speech is
> such observation and record as would note carefully the original sense
> to the child of his words, and the gradual *differentiation* of the original
> protoplasmic verbal-nominal-interjectional forms . . . . until words
> assume their present rigidity.

Another reason why the proportion of nouns in these early vocabularies may be too high is that the investigators, in many cases, engaged the child in conversation, endeavoring to bring out words that the child was thought to know. This type of investigation frequently took the form of asking the child to name objects. Obviously the proportion of nouns obtained by this procedure would be too high. Still other investigators have used a dictionary when searching for words that might be in the child's vocabulary. In the light of Kirkpatrick's [36] findings, this method would also tend to make the proportion of nouns too high. He reports that of the words in the dictionary, 60 per cent are nouns, 22 per cent adjectives, 11 per cent verbs, and 5.5 per cent adverbs; whereas using *Robinson Crusoe* as a sample of running vocabulary he finds 45 per cent nouns, 17 per cent adjectives, 24 per cent verbs, and 7 per cent adverbs. He reminds us also that ·in small vocabularies the proportions for the different parts of speech are quite different. Drever [21] brings out the effect of environment on the composition of the vocabulary. His conclusions are based not only on observations made on his own three children, but on observations of some slum children as well. He points out the problem, as it is indicated in the literature, in the following words:

Most students of the growth of language in children have asserted that the child starts with a vocabulary composed mainly of nouns. . . . . If this is true, we are faced with this difficulty as regards nearly every recorded vocabulary of children, that by two and a half the verbs occupy a much greater proportion of the vocabulary, relatively to the nouns, than in the case of the adult, and there must therefore come a time when the tendency is in the opposite direction.

He says that Boyd reports, "The tendency for verbs to increase relatively to nouns goes on at least to the age of four; according .to ours, the opposite tendency is already very pronounced at the age of three and a half." He maintains, on the basis of his investigations, that the large proportion of nouns is clearly due to a broader environment. In this connection, we must remember that most of the published vocabularies have been recorded for children who have had exceptional advantages in that they have been members of professional families, and frequently have had opportunity to travel, or in other ways have had environments conducive to the acquisition of new words, and particularly of nouns. Drever [21] then formulates a general principle in the growth of children's vocabularies as follows:

> That expansion of a child's environment always tends to increase nouns relatively to other parts of speech. Conversely, with a constant or relatively constant environment, the other parts of speech will increase relatively to the nouns. . . . . Whether increase of verbs relatively to nouns can be taken as a symptom of mental growth, we have no evidence before us to determine. Obviously, such an increase might simply be due to the environment remaining comparatively constant . . . . but there might, of course, be an additional tendency in this direction due to mental growth. We cannot help, however, expressing our frank scepticism regarding any such tendency. If we were to examine this general analysis of vocabularies for genuine symptoms of mental growth and development, we should look rather to the conjunctions and, in a less degree, to the pronouns.

In conclusion, the same author remarks that there are three factors that influence the development of the vocabulary, namely, environment, interest, and mental growth. "Environment," he says, "affects the nouns, interest affects the verbs, and mental grip is shown by pronouns, adverbs, prepositions, and conjunctions."

PARTS OF SPEECH IN CONVERSATION

These percentages of the different parts of speech in the total vocabulary of the child, in so far as we are able to determine them, are very interesting, but it seems that another important approach has received very little attention. Why should we not concern ourselves rather with the percentages of the various parts of speech in the child's running conversation? After all, it is in the child's conversation that he puts his vocabulary into use, and why should we not study the vocabulary as it is applied, rather than as a sort of mythical whole that is never used at one time? The total number of words in the dictionary determines the percentages of the different parts of speech that it is possible to know, and while every adult probably knows a great many more nouns than any other one type of word, the mechanism of sentence formation is such that only a small proportion of the fund of nouns is needed in conversation. Pronouns, verbs, and adjectives also come in as very important elements in language, as do also the connective words, and the words that express relations between the main words of a sentence. The method proposed results in striking differences. It seems that the method of considering the percentages in conversation is of much more practical value. Even when running conversation is considered, there are two methods of analysis that bring out striking differences. This is shown very clearly in the recent study by Zyve.[79] She used third grade children and recorded their conversation in a little story period of fifteen minutes each day for about three months. She tabulated her results by each of these methods, namely, by the variety or number of different words used, and by the frequency of the various parts of speech, based on the total number of words used. Her figures as presented here have been converted into percentages in order to bring out the relationships more clearly. Considering the variety of words used, the percentage of nouns is 51, while considering the total number of words used, it drops to 15 per cent. Verbs represent 22 per cent of the number of different words used, and they increase to 27 per cent of the total number of words. One of the artificialities of the method of using the variety of words is shown by the articles. There are only three articles in the English language; all three of them are used by the children, but they represent only .1 of 1 per cent of the number of different words. Yet we must recognize the importance of these words, and how frequently they are needed, and do occur in our conversation. When we use the total number of words used by the children in Zyve's [79] study, the percentage for the articles mounts to approximately 7 per cent. Probably the greatest change that occurs by this translation into different terms, in addition to the change in the nouns, is that of the pronouns, which show a relative increase from 1.5 per cent to 17.2 per cent. Similarly we note increases in the percentages of adverbs from 5 per cent to 9 per cent, of prepositions from 1 per cent to 8 per cent, and of conjunctions from .5 per cent to nearly 7 per cent. Like the nouns, the adjectives show a relative decrease when considered according to the total number of words used.

LANGUAGE TESTS

A little work has been done in an attempt to get tests of linguistic development. Smith [61] has evolved a very good vocabulary test in which words are elicited, either by a standard set of questions, or by showing pictures and objects where possible. Some of her conclusions on the basis of this test, which by using the odd-even method gave a reliability of +.97, are as follows:

The average number of words in children's vocabularies increases from 0 at eight months to about 2,500 at six years. The most significant factor in increase of vocabulary is that of mental age. Girls are likely to begin the acquisition of a vocabulary at an earlier age than boys, but the sex factor is not important after three years of age. It is probable that children of a higher social class have larger vocabularies than children of a lower social class even when mental ability is equal. Order of birth does not have any significance in the size of vocabulary after two and one-half years.

Descoeudres [16] has also devised a test that she calls a language test, which probably is simply an intelligence test with more of the tests involving verbal instructions and verbal responses. The test involves such tasks as comprehension and execution of commands, a phonetic test or a test of articulation in which the children were required to repeat words, a test of verbal memory, a vocabulary test, a test in which they were to name various objects, materials, colors, occupations and the like, and a test of verbal intelligence involving opposites and comparisons. The study is an excellent one and yields some very interesting results, but the whole battery of tests can hardly be called a language test. It is really quite similar to our intelligence tests. The author obtains a language age that probably is mental age as determined on her test. There are no consistent sex differences that appear in the study, but there are very marked and very consistent differences in favor of the upper social classes.

Piaget [56] has recently made a novel approach to the problem of child language, in which he emphasizes the function of the response in relation to the child's environment. His data were collected by observing two children, six and seven years of age, while they were engaged in free play at school. While the material is not adequate for scientific purposes, his method of analysis is most interesting and stimulating. As a modification of his method of analysis has been used in the present study, it will be presented in more detail in later chapters.

CHAPTER II

METHOD AND RELIABILITY

PURPOSE

The present investigation is an attempt to add to our knowledge of the development of the language of the child, as it is found in samples of the running conversation of a large number of children selected so as to give a random sampling of the population. The function of language in the child's life, the changes in the length of sentences, the complexity of sentence structure, and the proportion of the various parts of speech that occur in the material, are the chief aspects of the problem attacked in this investigation.

COLLECTION OF DATA

SUBJECTS

1. *Age.*—On the basis of several indications in the literature, it was decided to include in the present study children between the ages of eighteen and fifty-four months. While many writers report that children talk much earlier than the lower age limit of this experiment, it must be remembered that most of the reports in the literature are records of children of the professional class and are records of the most precocious members of that group. Eighteen months was taken as the significant age at which to begin this study of sentence formation, since it is the age at which the most advanced children begin to combine words.

Many writers report that by five years the child's conversation is so fluent that an accurate record of it for any great length of time is almost an impossibility. Nice [50] reports that the development of the sentence is practically complete by fifty-four months. It has not at that time reached the degree of perfection found in the adult, but the period of its most rapid development is over. It thus seems that in considering the language development of the small child we are dealing with a function which develops ve.y rapidly during the pre-school period, and which varies greatly from one individual to another as to the time of its appearance.

For the present study, therefore, twenty children were selected at each of the seven age levels of 18, 24, 30, 36, 42, 48, and 54 months, making a total of 140 subjects. These seven groups were absolutely discrete as to age, as each child was observed within a month and a half of the age at which he was classified. This method of selection meant that a child who was born on April 15, 1923, had to be examined between March 1 and June 1, 1926, in order to be included in the thirty-six-month-old group. The greatest discrepancy included was one of forty-eight days, and there were only four cases in which the deviation from the proper date for examination was more than forty days. An effort was made to have these deviations not in excess of two weeks for the children at the two youngest age levels, where development is most rapid. These differences, however, practically canceled each other, since the average ages for each group deviated very slightly from the exact date as shown in Table I.

In such a rigid stratification of age levels, this study differs markedly from previous investigations, particularly from that of Smith,[61] who examined the children first without regard to age and classified them later into convenient intervals, which in most cases were whole-year age groups. In her study, a three-year-old subject was any child between the ages of two years and six months, and three years and five months, so that her age groups were really not discrete but continuous. When we are dealing with a function that develops as rapidly as does the child's language, it seems that whole-year age groups are so large, and have so much variation within them, that the stages of the developmental process may be obscured.

2. *Paternal Occupation.*—In order to make the experimental group representative of the preschool population of Minneapolis, the occupation of the father was used as a criterion of selection. The Barr-Taussig sixfold classification of occupations, used by Goodenough,[27] was applied to the

TABLE I

MEAN DEVIATION FROM PROPER DATE FOR EXAMINATION

AGE* GROUP	DEVIATION IN DAYS
18	+ 2.9
24	— 7.5
30	— .9
36	+ 1.3
42	— 1.8
48	— 3.7
54	— .7

* In months.

adult male population of Minneapolis between the ages of twenty-one and forty-five years, and the percentage in each type of occupation was calculated from the census report of Minneapolis for the year 1920. These figures, together with the corresponding ones for the experimental group, are shown in Table II.

The subjects of the experimental group were carefully selected so that these socio-economic classes were represented in their proper proportions (see Table II, and Fig. I), not only in the group as a whole, but within each age level as well. Similarly the two sexes were approximately equally distributed in the entire group and in each age group.

TABLE II

Distribution of Cases by Age, Sex, and Paternal Occupation

	Professional		Managerial		Clerical		Skilled Labor		Semi-Skilled Labor		Unskilled Labor	
Occupational Group	I		II		III		IV		V		VI	
Per cent adult male population of Minneapolis	5.4		6.3		37.3		24.3		14.9		11.8	
Per cent total experimental group	5.0		6.4		35.7		25.7		15.7		11.4	

Sex

CA *	B	G	B	G	B	G	B	G	B	G	B	G
18	1	...	...	2	2	5	3	2	1	2	2	...
24	...	1	...	1	3	4	2	3	2	2	1	1
30	...	1	1	...	4	3	1	4	...	3	2	1
36	1	...	1	1	2	5	3	2	1	2	2	1
42	...	1	1	1	4	3	3	2	2	1	2	1
48	1	...	...	1	3	5	3	2	1	2	1	...
54	1	...	...	1	3	4	6	...	...	3	1	1

*In this and succeeding tables the chronological age is based upon the age in months.

27

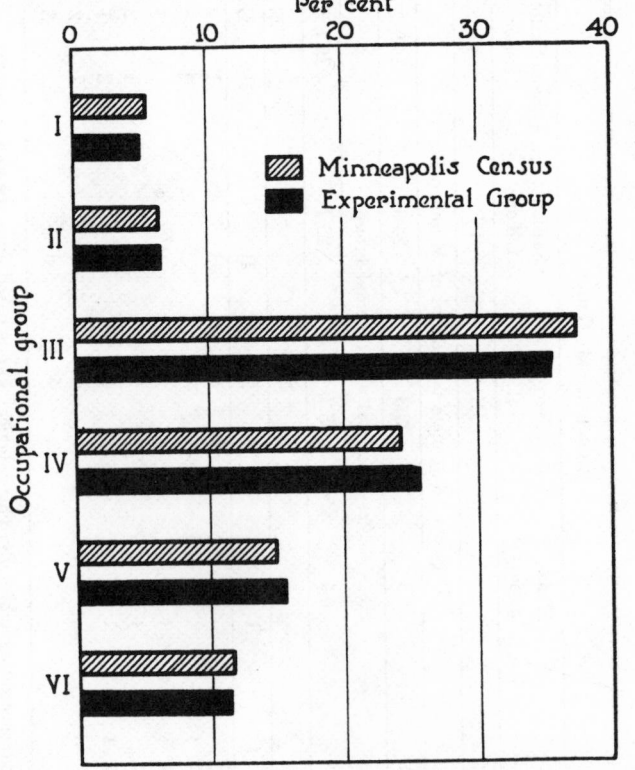

Fig. 1
Distribution of Cases by Paternal Occupation

3. *Intelligence.*—Mental test records, nearly all of which were based on the Kuhlmann Revision of the Binet Scale, were available on 95 per cent of the subjects.*

The mean IQ for each age group is decidedly above 100, as is shown in Table III. However, this does not mean that the group is as highly selected as the figures seem to indicate, for it must be remembered that Kuhlmann's original standardization gave average IQ's of 108, 106, and 107 for the ages of two, three, and four years, respectively. The corresponding figures from the Goodenough [27] restandardization of the Kuhlmann scale are given in the same table. It will be seen from a comparison of these figures that in spite of the rigid method of selection used in this study, in an attempt to secure a random sampling of the preschool population of Minneapolis, the experimental group was slightly above the average in intelligence at each age level. This tendency, it will be seen, is more marked in the girls than it is in the boys, which is in accordance with the findings of Goodenough [27] and others. These sex differences will be discussed in more detail in Chapter VII.

The mean IQ for each occupational group is shown in Table IV, together with the corresponding figures from the Goodenough [27] study. It will be seen that while in general they seem somewhat higher, they are in the same order of magnitude except for the one high mean of Group II.

Although the method of selection used in this experiment is the best that we now know, certain unknown selective factors have been operative in spite of our precautions, which might

*Four of these records were based on the new Minnesota Intelligence Test for Preschool Children. These scores were translated into terms of IQ in the treatment of the data. The remaining 5 per cent of the children for whom no mental test records could be obtained have been considered as having the mean mental age of the chronological age group to which each belonged.

TABLE III

Mean IQ's by Age and Sex According to Two Standardizations and in the Experimental Group

CA	Goodenough (Original Kuhlmann Test)			Kuhlmann	Experimental Group		
	Boys	Girls	All	All	Boys	Girls	All
18	......	......	......	......	109.8	113.7	112.0
24	104.3	105.9	105.1	108.0	106.7	115.3	111.9
30	......	......	......	......	106.0	103.7	104.6
36	100.7	108.1	104.4	106.0	101.2	105.8	103.3
42	......	......	......	......	106.6	111.1	108.4
48	104.7	114.1	109.4	107.0	106.5	117.9	112.8
54	......	......	......	......	102.6	121.0	110.9

bring about the slightly higher intelligence rating of these children. One of the factors is the cooperation of the parents. No parents refused to allow observation of their children for this experiment, but the families with whom contact was made were largely either those whose children were members of the control group of the Institute of Child Welfare at the University of Minnesota, and who had been brought to the

TABLE IV

Mean IQ by Paternal Occupation

Occupational Group	This Study	Goodenough (Original Kuhlmann Test)
I. Professional	118.1	116.1
II. Managerial	121.0	111.7
III. Clerical	112.0	107.7
IV. Skilled labor	105.9	105.3
V. Semiskilled labor	106.4	104.3
VI. Unskilled labor	100.3	96.0

Institute at least once for mental examination, or those who had availed themselves of the opportunities of the free clinics of the Infant Welfare Society of Minneapolis. These two factors probably operated to make the selection somewhat too high. A similar factor was operative in the opposite direction among the members of the lower occupational groups, since they were recruited chiefly from institutions and from the clients of social agencies. A third of these factors is the greater stability of the population from which the subjects were selected, since only those whose addresses were the same for several months, or a year, were available for observation. Thus, while we still have some errors of selection, they tend to counteract each other, and the experimental group in this study is probably as good a sampling as it is practically possible to secure.

METHOD OF OBSERVATION

Each child was observed individually in his own home or in a place very familiar to him, such as a room in the Nursery School or in one of the day nurseries of which the child was a member. Whenever possible, the child was alone in the room with the examiner, but in making home visits this condition was often difficult to control. In many cases the mother was present during all or part of the observation, and this circumstance often put the child more at ease. Occasionally, other members of the family were present as well, which factor usually stimulated the child's conversation rather than hindered it.

Fifty consecutive verbal responses were recorded for each child exactly as they sounded to the experimenter. This number was decided upon because it would give a fairly representative sample of the child's stage of linguistic development in a relatively short period of time, without tiring the child with a prolonged observation. A response was considered as a separate unit if it was marked off from the preceding and succeeding remarks by pauses. A complete sentence was always considered as a single response, but a response was frequently less than a sentence. The responses were recorded exactly as they sounded to the experimenter, even in the cases of the youngest children, many of whom gave verbal responses that were entirely incomprehensible. However, these children have many sounds in their vocal repertoires for which we have no adequate written symbols; and hence, any attempt to record their utterances in writing is very unsatisfactory. Such responses have been treated separately, and the only accurate result they yield is the number of syllables combined per response. In some cases of peculiar articulation, the mother's interpretation was considered if it clarified the child's speech, and if it was obvious that she was giving a literal reproduction and was not elaborating on what the child had said. It was surprising, however, in how many of these cases the mother was quite frank in admitting that she understood the child no better than did the examiner. The record did not include recitation of nursery rhymes from memory or responses uttered in direct imitation of another person.

In order to overcome self-consciousness and to establish rapport, the child was shown picture-books and toys, which usually were quite effective as an introduction. The same set of toys was used throughout the experiment. One of the picture-books contained pictures of animals, usually with one central object in each picture. This book was particularly suitable for the younger subjects, who could not comprehend the group relations (Stern [63]) in more complicated pictures. Another book which was used, and which was more suitable for the older children, contained group pictures illustrating various Mother Goose rhymes. The toys used were a little red auto, a cat that squeaked, a telephone with a bell, a little tin mouse, a music box, and a small ball. The toys were not presented in the same order to all children. Frequently, the older children were asked whether they preferred to look at toys or picture-books first. A preference was usually indicated, but if not, the experimenter presented the toy that seemed best suited to the age, sex, and apparent interest of the child. If it failed to bring forth any verbal responses after considerable inspection on the part of the child, another toy was tried. Sometimes a child became so fascinated with the first or second toy that the quota of fifty responses was obtained without the presentation of other toys. Some of the children, on the other hand, flitted from one object to another so rapidly, and with so few comments, that the whole series was gone through several times before the desired number of responses was obtained.

Since the aim was to secure spontaneous responses, the child was addressed as little as possible during the observation. In the cases of some quiet, shy children, it was necessary to stimulate conversation to some extent, but an effort was made, in such cases, not to use questions that could be answered by a single word. If the child's response was brought about by something the examiner or the mother had said, it was recorded as an *elicited response* and, where necessary, the remark of the other person was also recorded verbatim. This method of recording differs from those used by Piaget,[56] Smith,[61] and others in three ways: first, the child is talking to an adult, rather than playing with children; second, the same amount of data is obtained for each child; ánd third, the situation is more nearly the same for all subjects. Piaget[56] and Smith[61] observed the children for a definite period of time during free play in groups with other children. The situations differed greatly from one child to another, for in some cases the children were engaged in active play outdoors, while in other cases they were engaged in quiet, indoor play in which conversation was much greater in quantity and probably different in quality. In observing children for a definite length of time, as was done in these other studies, very few data were obtained from some quiet, shy subjects, while a tremendous amount of material was obtained from the talkative ones. It seems that it is better to compare equal samplings of children's language responses recorded in similar circumstances, even though the situation may not be entirely natural.

In the Piaget[56] study and in the Smith[61] study, the person with whom the child conversed was different for each observation, and often changed during an observation; whereas, in the present study all the children conversed with the same person, thus standardizing this aspect of the experimental situation.

Other data obtained for all the subjects of the experiment included: the length of time required to secure the fifty responses; the time of the observation (appointments were made at times that would not interfere with the children's usual nap hours); the nationality of the parents, if they were of foreign birth; whether or not the child heard a foreign language in the home; the age of the child's associates; and whether the child had lived chiefly in the home or in an institution.

ANALYSIS OF DATA

In any attempt to deal with data of this sort, one is immediately confronted with a great many difficulties. Everyone who has tried to understand the chatter of little ones realizes from this casual observation how difficult it is to hear the child's words correctly. Children of eighteen and twenty-four months vocalize a great deal, and whether we understand them or not, we cannot afford to ignore these important stages in their linguistic development. Even children who can be readily understood most of the time, frequently use words and phrases that are entirely unintelligible to the hearer. It was necessary, therefore, to divide the data of this experiment into: (1) *comprehensible responses,* which included all responses that could be understood by the experimenter in spite of poor articulation, letter substitutions, or faulty or incomplete construction; (2) *semicomprehensible responses,* which included all responses in which the hearer had a general idea of what the child was talking about but could not get the full meaning because of the lack of certain key words in the sentence; and (3) *incomprehensible vocalization,* which included all responses which were mere sounds forming no recognizable words, and which were entirely devoid of meaning to the hearer. These responses included three sub-groups: *(a) single sound; (b) repetition of the same sound,* or *babbling;* and *(c) series of varied sounds.*

ANALYSIS ACCORDING TO THE LENGTH OF RESPONSE

The only quantitative treatment of these data in terms of equal units that is possible, is the analysis according to the length of response. The semicomprehensible responses and the incomprehensible vocalization were scored according to the number of syllables combined per response, while the comprehensible responses were scored by the number of words per response. In attempting to count the number of words in a response, many problems arise as to what is to be considered a separate word and what combinations are to be counted as one word. In order to overcome these difficulties and to standardize this part of the scoring system, it was necessary to formulate a set of arbitrary rules, as follows:

1. Contractions of the subject and predicate like "it's," "we're," "you're," etc., were scored as two words. In such cases the child speaks correctly according to adult conversational usage, which really is his only model of correct speech. Each part of the contraction is an essential part of the sentence, and if the sentence is to be considered complete, it is necessary to recognize these two parts. In order, therefore, to make the analysis according to the length of response consistent with the later analysis according to the construction of the response, it seemed justifiable to score such contractions as two separate words.

2. Contractions of the verb and the negative like "can't," "won't," etc., were scored as single words. The child who has no knowledge of how words are written does not know that "can't" is a contraction of "can" and "not." He hears "can" as one word and "can't" as another; they have different

meanings and hence are probably two distinct and independent words to the child.

3. Hyphenated words and compound nouns, particularly proper nouns, which are not hyphenated, but which probably function as single words and as names of single objects, were scored as one word. For example, "merry-go-round," "Mother Goose," "Betty Lou," and such expressions were scored as single words.

4. Each part of a verbal combination was scored as a separate word. For example, "have been playing" counted as three words.

5. "Lookit," which occurred frequently, was scored as one word if it was used alone and functioned simply as "look." If, however, it was followed by an object, it was counted as the two words "look at."

FUNCTIONAL ANALYSIS

Language is the foundation of all our social relations, for it is the primary medium by which we communicate our ideas and meaning to others. Dewey [18] says that the primary motive of language is to influence the activity of others. Its secondary use is to enter into more intimate social relations with them, and the third and final use of language is in the acquisition of knowledge. Thus, this important aspect of the child's language develops in relation to the needs of the child. In considering the linguistic development of the young child, we should concern ourselves not only with its increasing length and complexity of structure but with its function in relation to the child's environment. What situations in which the child is placed bring about language responses? We find the young infant very early expressing himself in gestures, but when he begins to substitute verbal responses for his overt bodily responses, which overt responses are first superseded by verbal responses? In what situations does speech first appear?

Piaget [56] considers this a problem of functional psychology, which indeed it is. Sometimes, he says, language conveys information, sometimes it provokes action in others, etc. This is an important aspect of the linguistic development of the young child that heretofore has been quite neglected. The old grammatical classification of sentences into declarative, interrogative, imperative, and exclamatory sentences is a crude analysis in this direction, which serves fairly well for written language, less well for adult conversation, and is quite inadequate when applied to the speech of children. As Claparède so aptly says in the preface of Piaget's book, "In examining child thought, we have applied to it the mould and pattern of the adult mind."

So often a sentence is structurally of one kind and functionally of another; there is so much overlapping of the categories; and so many subheads would have been necessary to make it meet the demands of children's conversation, that the rigid grammatical classification of sentences was abandoned in the present study. The function of the child's response in relation to his environment was considered the important thing in this type of approach. Practically the only attempt at treatment of this sort, that is available in the literature, is that of Jean Piaget [56] of the Jean Jacques Rousseau Institute at Geneva. He says in the introductory chapter, "We have aimed first and foremost at creating a method which could be applied to fresh observations and lead to a comparison of results." This method has filled a serious need in the present study very satisfactorily, and has been adopted with certain modifications in the functional analysis of the data. Modifications of the classification were made necessary by the different circumstances under which the observations were made, by the use of much younger subjects, and by the desirability of subdividing some of the larger categories for a more detailed analysis. All of the comprehensible responses were scored according to this functional analysis, which, as modified for the present purposes, consisted of the following categories:

A. Egocentric speech
    1. Repetition or echolalia
    2. Monologue
    3. Dual or collective monologue

B. Socialized speech
    1. Adapted information
        (a) Naming
        (b) Remarks about the immediate situation
        (c) Remarks associated with the situation
        (d) Irrelevant remarks
    2. Criticism
    3. Emotionally toned responses
    4. Questions
    5. Answers
    6. Social phrases
    7. Dramatic imitation

By *egocentric speech* Piaget [56] means that in which the audience is disregarded. The child "talks either for himself or for the pleasure of associating any one who happens to be there with the activity of the moment." He "speaks only about himself and makes no attempt to place himself at the point of view of his hearer." In this study this category includes instances in which the child speaks about persons and things other than himself, but in which he disregards an audience. The three types of egocentric *speech* are defined as follows: *Repetition* or *echolalia* means "repetition of words and syllables. . . . for the pleasure of talking, with no thought of talking to anyone, nor even at times of saying words that will make sense." *Monologue* occurs when the child "talks to himself as though he were thinking aloud" without addressing anyone. In the third type, called *dual or collective mono-*

logue, "an outsider is always associated with the action or thought of the moment but is expected neither to hear nor to understand. The point of view of the hearer is never taken into account. His presence serves only as a stimulus. . . . . The child talks about himself without collaboration with his audience or without evoking a dialogue."

Socialized speech occurs when the child addresses his hearer, or considers his point of view, tries to influence him, or actually exchanges ideas with his hearer. The first category of socialized speech according to Piaget[56] is *adapted information*, in which the child really "exchanges his thoughts with others, either by telling him something that will interest him, influence his actions, or by actual interchange of ideas." It occurs whenever "the child adopts the point of view of his hearer, and when the latter is not chosen at random." This group was found to include such a large proportion of the conversation obtained in this experiment, that it seemed advisable to analyze it in more detail. The first subgroup that appears to be quite distinct is that of *naming*, in which the child announces the name of an object either as a single word or in a complete sentence. The second type includes all *remarks about the immediate situation*, other than naming. The third group is made up of all remarks that are not about the immediate situation but are logically related to it, i.e., where the observer can see the connection between events or remarks in the situation. For example, if upon presentation of a toy auto the child said, "It's a auto," the response would be placed in the naming group. If his next remark was, "It's got a spare tire," this remark would belong in the second type of adapted information, or the remarks about the immediate situation. If the succeeding remarks were, "I have a car like that," "Mine's broken," they would be additional information volunteered by the child, which was obviously brought about by the situation and associated with it, and hence belong in the third type of adapted information, or *remarks associated with the situation.* The fourth type of adapted information consists of *irrelevant remarks;* that is, those in which the observer cannot notice any connection with previous remarks or actions.

The second type of socialized speech is *criticism,* which includes "all remarks about the work or behavior of others, but having the same character as adapted information," according to Piaget's [56] definition. In the present analysis, this classification was extended to include criticisms of objects as well as that of persons and also complaints about situations in which the child is thwarted.

In the third group of socialized speech, Piaget [56] includes all "commands, requests, and threats." For the present purposes, this category has been extended to include all wish-words or "Wunsch-wortes" as Meumann [45] terms them—in short, this group includes all *emotionally toned responses.* Single-word sentences uttered with a decided emotional or commanding inflection are also included in this group.

The fourth group consists of *questions,* by which are meant real interrogative sentences with an interrogative function and declarative sentences having an interrogative function, i.e., any remark that definitely requires an answer from the hearer. It does not include declarative sentences with a question added at the end merely for affirmation or approval of the statement and requiring no answer on the part of the hearer, as "I made it go, didn't I?"

In the fifth group are included all *answers* that are "answers to real questions and to commands." In this study the category includes all of the elicited responses. However, remarks occurring in the course of conversation and having the form of answers, but which are answers to remarks that are not questions, are not placed in this category but rather under adapted information.

A sixth category has been added to Piaget's [56] classification to provide for the *social phrases* which occur only in social situations, but which the child has been taught to say parrot-fashion, and which probably function as single words to the child, such as, "please," "thank you," "you are welcome," "bye-bye," etc.

The last group of socialized speech is called *dramatic imitation,* which consists of all talk in imitation of the conversation of adults, like imaginary imitative telephone conversations. It also includes imitation of the sounds made by animals, like "bow-wow-wow," "meow," "moo-moo," and the imitation of the sounds of automobile horns, etc. Probably Piaget [56] would put such remarks in one of the categories of egocentric speech, but while many such remarks might be placed there, some of them are used in decidedly social situations and in social contexts, and hence this classification has been provided for them in this study.

Construction Analysis

We have now outlined two methods of analysis of these data, both of which consider the response as a whole. The first was a quantitative analysis based on the length of response and the second was a functional analysis of the response according to its relation to the child's environment or to the total situation. There is still another important aspect of the development of speech that must be considered. This is an analysis according to the construction of the response, which attempts to indicate the stage of grammatical complexity that the child has reached, or in other words, how closely his sentence structure approximates adult conversation, his sole criterion upon which to model his speech.

The first and most obvious way to classify responses of this sort is to throw them into the dichotomy of *complete* versus *incomplete* sentences, and these are the two main groups of this type of analysis. However, in a preliminary perusal of these data, one is impressed with the frequency of responses that are incomplete sentences. Ordinarily, we think that we speak in complete sentences, and that the sentence is the essential unit of language. A superficial analysis of a small sample of adult conversation is sufficient, however, to show that a large proportion of our conversation is composed of phrases and other groups of words that really do not constitute sentences according to the grammarian's definition. Very often the whole sentence is merely implied or "understood" as the grammarians say, but it is not expressed in its full form. True, the adult understands that a verb and a subject belong in a sentence, and were he to write the same statement, he would use the complete form. But the child knows nothing of written language; his sole pattern and criterion of correctness of language is the conversation of the adults with whom he associates. If a response is adequate in the situation, and is what an adult would say in such circumstances, the child is using the most complete form that he has had an opportunity to learn, and therefore, in this study such responses have been classified separately as one type of complete response that is *functionally complete but structurally incomplete.* This group, then, includes practically all the single-word sentences and most of the elicited responses or those belonging in the answers group of the functional analysis. The outline of the classification used in this third type of analysis is as follows:

A. Complete Responses
   1. Functionally complete but structurally incomplete responses
   2. Simple sentences without a phrase
   3. Simple sentences with a phrase
   4. Compound sentences
   5. Complex sentences
   6. Elaborated sentences

B. Incomplete Responses
  1. Omission of the verb
  2. Omission of the subject
  3. Omission of a preposition
  4. Omission of a conjunction
  5. Omission of the verb and the subject
  6. Miscellaneous omissions (itemized)

The titles of the second, third, fourth, and fifth categories of the *complete responses* are quite adequate and need no further explanation. The sixth classification, *elaborated sentences,* however, represents an interesting type of response that it seems advisable to include as a separate group. In scoring the responses of some of the oldest children, it was noticed that they often used long, involved sentences that really were much more complex and seemed to indicate a higher stage of linguistic development than the ordinary compound and complex sentences, which, in some cases, may be quite short. This classification was added, therefore, in order to differentiate these more involved responses and to see if they proved diagnostic of a more advanced stage of development. This group includes sentences with two phrases, two clauses, or a phrase and a clause.

All responses that were incomplete functionally as well as structurally were scored as *incomplete,* and the type of omission was indicated. The major groups of omission are shown in the above outline. Other combinations of omissions occurred but not with sufficient frequency to warrant separate analysis. These, therefore, are the groups that are included in the miscellaneous omissions. Since in recording children's speech it is often difficult to be sure whether or not one hears the articles, omissions of the articles have been disregarded. If a sentence was complete except for an article, it was considered complete and no penalty was inflicted for its omission, since its absence might have been a function of the recording and not a true omission on the part of the child. It was possible to give construction scores only to comprehensible responses and to the more complete of the semicomprehensible responses. Thus, we have outlined three types of analysis that deal with the response as a whole, namely: the length analysis, which is quantitative; and the functional and construction analyses, which are qualitative.

Word Analysis

In addition to the above-described analyses that consider the response as a whole, it was thought advisable, particularly for comparison with the numerous vocabulary studies reported in the literature, to conduct a more detailed analysis by considering the parts of the response. Hence, although the primary purpose of this study was to study the development of the sentence and to consider the response as a whole, a word analysis has also been conducted. The vocabulary reports in the literature are much more thorough than that of the present study, in that they are based on more complete samples of each child's vocabulary. However, as mentioned in Chapter I, these studies have all been of two or three children, all at different age levels, so that data for comparisons of children of the same age, and for tracing the changes from one age to another, are very meager. This word analysis has been conducted merely to see if small samples of the vocabularies of a large number of children would confirm the reports of the complete vocabularies of a few children, and in order to suggest possible tentative, normative material on the proportions of the different parts of speech at the various age levels. As mentioned in the preceding chapter, there are nearly as many ways of counting children's vocabularies and for determining the proportions of the various parts of speech as there are writers on the subject. However, Bateman's [5] rules for counting words and for determining the parts of speech seem to have met with favor from other authors (Hull and Quitzi [32] and Nice [51]), and since they have been used in three or four other studies, they have been applied in the present instance. They are as follows:

1. Include no proper nouns.

2. Include no plural form unless the singular was not used.

3. Include all forms of pronouns.

4. Include no variants of verbs or of adjectives unless they are from a different root.

5. The same word may be listed more than once according to its grammatical use; i.e., if a word is used as a noun and also as a verb, it is included twice.

The frequency of occurrence of each word was found as well as the total number of words, the total number of different words, and the percentage of each part of speech used at each age level.

RELIABILITY

At first sight the method described above may seem to be quite subjective and may seem to warrant the frequent charge made against material of this sort, namely, that of unreliability. In order to check the justifiability of such a charge, the reliability of this method has been studied in two different ways.

RELIABILITY OF THE CHILDREN'S RESPONSES

This was obtained by correlating the odd- with the even-numbered responses in order to see how consistently the children used responses of a certain length, and how consistently they used the responses in the various larger categories of the functional and construction classifications. All the coefficients by the odd-even method have been corrected by the use of the Spearman-Brown formula, $\dfrac{2r}{1 + r}$. The mean reliability coefficient for the analysis according to the length of response was $+.91$, the range being from $+.82$ to $+.97$ for the various age levels. The corresponding odd-even reliability coefficients for the most important items in the functional and construction analyses are shown in Table V.

TABLE V

MEAN RELIABILITY COEFFICIENTS FOR VARIOUS ITEMS
OF EACH TYPE OF ANALYSIS

	SCORING	ODD-EVEN
Length of response	$+.99$	$+.91$
Functional analysis		
Egocentric responses	....	$+.89$
Naming	$+.68$	$+.87$
Remarks about immediate situation	$+.73$	$+.81$
Remarks associated with the situation	$+.73$	$+.88$
Emotionally toned responses	$+.81$	$+.74$
Questions	$+.84$	$+.85$
Answers	$+.90$	$+.88$
Construction analysis		
Functionally complete but structurally incomplete	$+.94$	$+.92$
Simple sentences without a phrase	$+.95$	$+.87$
Simple sentences with a phrase	$+.91$	$+.59$
Omission of the verb	$+.57$	$+.75$
Omission of the subject	$+.97$	$+.64$

It will be seen from these figures that the reliability coefficients obtained by the odd-even method are all surprisingly high. Whenever they drop below $+.85$ it is because of the low frequency of these items, either throughout the group as a whole, or at certain age levels. No doubt, if more data had been collected, so that each type of response could have occurred with sufficient frequency to warrant statistical treatment and interpretation, all of the coefficients in this table would have been above +.85.

RELIABILITY OF THE METHOD OF SCORING

We have seen that the method of analysis described in the above sections proved to have high reliability as found by the odd-even method; i.e., that the children tended to use each type of response quite consistently. Let us now consider the reliability of this method from the point of view of the scorer. It may seem, at first sight, that any scorer using the definitions of the categories as they are given above, particularly those of the functional analysis, would be quite free to use his own subjective judgment in scoring the responses according to this method. Piaget [56] says:

> This classification, like any other, is open to the charge of artificiality. What is more important, however, is that it should stand the test of practical application; i.e., that any reader, who has made himself familiar with our criteria, should place the same phrases more or less in the same categories. Four people have been engaged in classifying the material in hand . . . . and the results of their respective enquiries were found to coincide within two or three per cent.

In the present study both the functional and construction classifications have been subjected to a similar test of practical application. Three other individuals, in addition to the experimenter, scored 10 per cent of the records independently. The records were chosen at random from each of the seven age levels. The scorers were given the rigid definitions of the various categories that were presented earlier in this chapter. The percentage of the responses placed in each category by each scorer was correlated (using the Spearman rank-order method) with that found by every other scorer. The averages of these coefficients of correlation are also shown in Table V.

We see that there was fairly close agreement among the scorers for material of this sort. In general, the correlations tended to run high, but the means presented above have been lowered somewhat by a few exceptionally low correlations that occurred as a result of certain misunderstandings of the directions. It is obvious that since every response had to be placed in some category of each type of classification, failure to place a response in its proper group meant that it was included in some other group, so that one mistake or misunderstanding of directions affected the correlations for two or more items. Another factor that entered in, tending to lower the correlations, was that one of the scorers apparently did the scoring less carefully than did the others and had greater disagreement with all the other scorers on certain items than they had with each other. The mean of the correlations for each scorer with each of the others on all the items combined was: Scorer A, +.83; Scorer B, +.84; Scorer C, +.79; Scorer D, +.81. This method probably could be improved with respect to this type of reliability by a few changes in the definitions, by way of making them more definite and more objective. This test has served merely as a preliminary indicator which shows that the method is reliable enough for use with groups, and in some instances meets Kelley's criterion for individual prediction (+.90). This test has been useful also in showing wherein the rules for scoring are weak, and just where improvement should be made. If longer samples of each child's conversation were obtained, so that the small categories would be better represented, and a few minor changes were made in the wording of the scoring rules, the reliability would be increased.

CHAPTER III

LENGTH OF RESPONSES

Most students of children's language in the past have been interested chiefly in the extent of vocabularies, that is, in how many words the children had in their active vocabularies. As mentioned in Chapter I, little interest has been evinced in the way children combine words into word groups, and finally, into complete sentences. The simplest and most objective measure of the degree to which children combine words at the various ages is the mean length of response. This measure has been advocated by Nice,[50] who says that it is not the occasional long sentence, but rather the mean length of response, which is symptomatic of the child's stage of linguistic development. Smith,[61] in her study carried on at the University of Iowa, also used this measure and found it a very satisfactory index.

As only the comprehensible responses could be treated according to this analysis, it will be well to consider here the percentage of the children's responses that were comprehensible at each age level. These results appear in Table VI.

It will be seen from these figures, that children's speech becomes increasingly comprehensible with increase in chronological age, that it is almost entirely comprehensible by the age of three or three and one-half years, and that this development occurs earlier in the girls than it does in the boys. Consequently, the number of responses upon which the figures to be reported in the later results are based is larger at the upper age levels. The smallest number of responses considered for any age level in this analysis is 260, while the largest

TABLE VI

MEAN PER CENT COMPREHENSIBLE RESPONSES
BY CA AND SEX

CA	BOYS	GIRLS	ALL
18	14.0	38.0	26.0
24	49.0	78.0	67.0
30	93.0	86.0	89.0
36	88.0	99.3	93.0
42	95.5	99.8	97.2
48	99.3	99.8	99.6
54	99.6	100.0	99.8

is 980 or practically the total number of responses obtained for the age level.

Several statistical measures of the length of response were compared for reliability. They were the mean length of response, the median length of response, the mean of the five longest responses, and the longest response for each child. The last two measures were eliminated because of their large variabilities.

It was thought for a time that the median length of response might be a better measure, in this case, because it seemed that many children used a preponderance of responses of one or two words and had a few very long sentences that would unduly affect the mean. The distributions of the mean and of the median length of response were compared with respect to their reliabilities, not only for the whole experimental group, but within each age group as well. Table VII shows the standard errors of the means and of the medians as determined by these formulae:

$$\sigma_M = \frac{\sigma_{dis}}{\sqrt{N}} \text{ and } \sigma_{Mdn.} \doteq \frac{i \sqrt{N}}{2f},$$

in which N represents the total number of comprehensible responses at each age level.

Although the difference in the reliability of the means and of the medians appears to be very slight, it is somewhat in favor of the mean as a more reliable index. The distributions according to the mean length of response and according to the

TABLE VII

STANDARD ERRORS OF THE MEAN AND OF THE MEDIAN LENGTH
OF RESPONSE FOR EACH CA GROUP

CA	MEAN	σ_M	$\sigma_{Mdn.}$
18	1.2	.022	.035
24	1.8	.055	.038
30	3.1	.067	.078
36	3.4	.068	.088
42	4.3	.091	.094
48	4.4	.091	.086
54	4.6	.094	.096

median length of response approximate the normal curve quite closely, especially when we consider that the number of cases involved is only 140. Some children did not talk at all, and so had a zero score for length of response, while some at the upper extreme, had a mean length of response of eight words. This fact might be interpreted to mean that the children used in this experiment were chosen at the proper ages, since with only a few children representing each extreme the distribution is nearly normal. The distribution according to the mean length of response, however, gives a closer approximation to the normal curve than that according to the median length of response. Therefore, in view of the facts that the standard error of the mean indicated that this measure was slightly more reliable, and that the distribution of the mean lengths of response gives a more nearly normal curve, the mean is the measure that has been used throughout the other tables of this chapter.

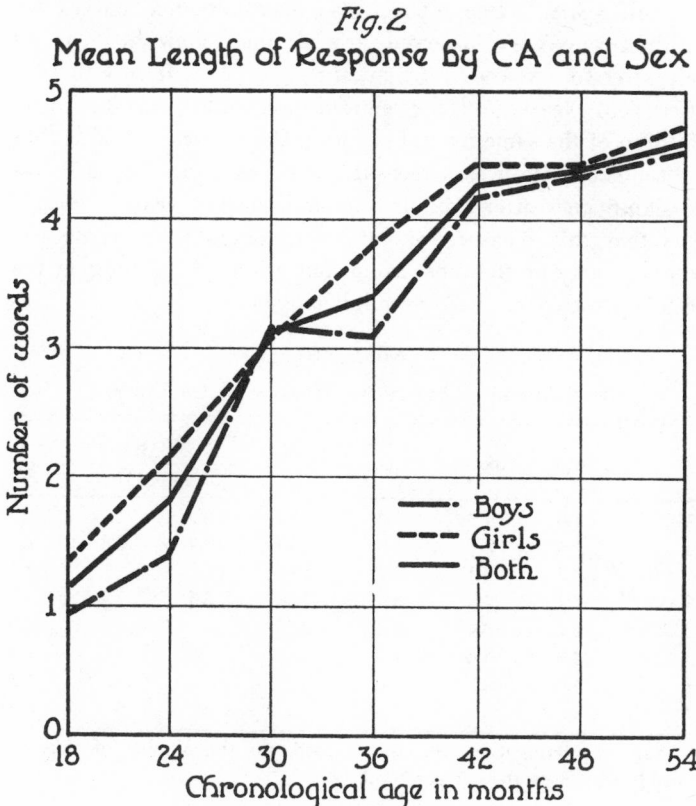

Fig.2

Mean Length of Response by CA and Sex

CHRONOLOGICAL AGE

The mean length of response shows consistent increase with advance in age (see Table VIII and Fig. 2), with the most rapid, increase between eighteen and forty-two months, and with a much slower increase after forty-two months. This result agrees with that of Smith,[61] who says regarding this measure, "There is a steady increase up to four and one-half years, with only small increments of gain after three and one-half years." She reports also that individual curves for children who were observed several times show little or no gain after four years. Further, she says, "This failure to gain after four years and the extreme variability in the older children of the same mental ability make it seem probable that the sentence length as a measure of sentence development has no significance after four or four and one-half years." Nice [50] says that this measure of the mean number of words per response may be the most important criterion for judging the child's progress in attaining adult language.

TABLE VIII

MEAN NUMBER OF WORDS PER RESPONSE BY CA AND SEX

CA	BOYS	GIRLS	ALL	SD*	SMITH'S FIGURES		
					Boys	Girls	All
18	1.0	1.3	1.2	.64	....	....	....
24	1.4	2.1	1.8	1.40	1.9	2.4	1.7
30	3.2	3.1	3.1	1.99	....	....	2.4
36	3.1	3.8	3.4	2.06	3.5	3.1	3.3
42	4.2	4.4	4.3	2.83	....	....	4.0
48	4.3	4.4	4.4	2.86	3.4	4.5	4.3
54	4.6	4.7	4.6	2.95	....	....	4.7
60	....	....	....	....	4.8	4.5	4.6

* In calculating the SD's, the N used was the number of comprehensible responses at each age level.

It will be seen from the above table, that the results of the present study tend to agree with those of the Smith [61] study, although they run somewhat higher for the group as a whole, especially at the lower age levels, and the sex differences are more marked. Her figures are also lower than those reported by Boyd,[7] Nice,[50] and others, which fact she attributes to the differences in the methods of collecting the data, namely, during "periods of lessened activity and conversation with adults." It must be remembered that this same factor of conversation with adults was operative in the present experiment, but the method in this case should be more reliable since the situation is more carefully standardized (see Chapter II).

SEX DIFFERENCES

Contrary to the results of the Smith[61] experiment, but quite in accordance with the findings of most other investigators, particularly those of Gale,[23] Mead,[43] Terman,[68] Nice,[48] and Doran,[20] this study reveals sex differences in favor of the girls which, though slight, are consistently in the same direction. There is only one slight reversal, which occurs in an age group in which there was a predominance of girls and in which the boys seem to have been rather highly selected in spite of the careful methods of selection that were used. In view of the consistency of these differences from one age level to another, their relationship to similar differences in the other analyses, and their agreement with the reports of other investigators, they should be considered as suggestive, and possibly significant, even though they do not meet the statistical criterion of the significance of a difference. It will be seen from inspection of the above table, that the differences are greater in the younger age levels at the time when the curve shows the most rapid rise, and that they are less marked in the older children, when development is slower. It seems to indicate that the girls go through the developmental cycle more rapidly than do the boys, but that the boys practically equal them at the close of this rapid developmental period. A similar tendency was noted by Doran[20] in studying vocabularies. He says, "We are not warranted in saying which has the better vocabulary after the twenty-fourth month, though

it is possible that further investigation will show the girls
surpass the boys up to the fifth or sixth year."

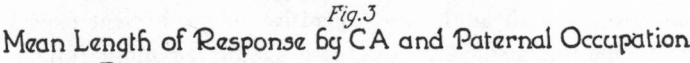

Fig.3
Mean Length of Response by CA and Paternal Occupation

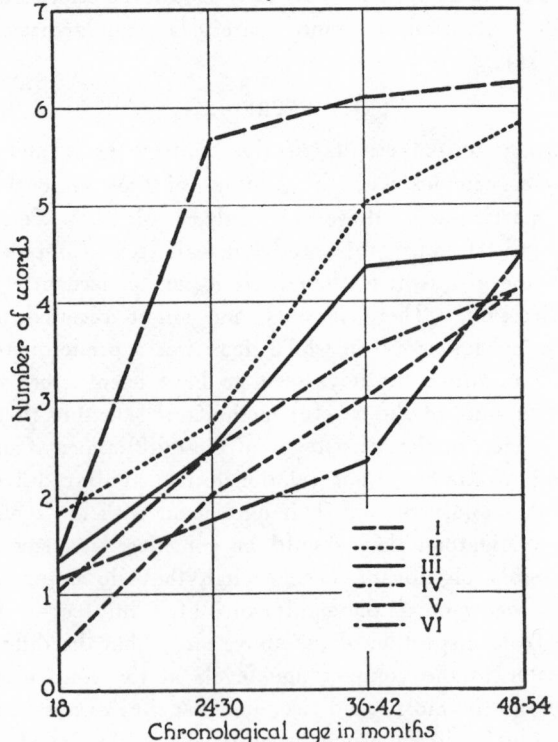

PATERNAL OCCUPATION

The mean length of response shows interesting trends when
considered in relation to paternal occupation. Because of the
small number of cases representing the extreme occupational
groups, the age levels have been considered in groups of two

in this part of the analysis. Table IX and Fig. 3 indicate a clear superiority of Group I over all the other occupational groups in the precocity of this aspect of linguistic develop- ment, and the other occupational groups appear in their expected positions at nearly all age levels. It will be noted that there is very little crossing of the curves for the various occupational groups, especially when we consider the few subjects in each group. The greatest crossing occurs in

TABLE IX

MEAN LENGTH OF RESPONSE BY CA AND PATERNAL OCCUPATION

CA	OCCUPATIONAL GROUP					
	I	II	III	IV	V	VI
18	1.4	1.8	1.3	1.0	.4	1.2
24 and 30	5.7	2.8	2.5	2.5	2.0	1.8
36 and 42	6.1	5.0	4.4	3.5	3.0	2.4
48 and 54	6.3	5.9	4.5	4.1	4.1	4.5

Group VI, which has fewer representatives than many of the other groups, about half of whom were secured through day nurseries or institutions, so that they had other contacts and other opportunities of hearing language outside of the home. Here we have one factor that might account for the crossing of this curve.

The mean length of sentence for Groups I, II, and III, has been compared with that for Groups IV, V, and VI, at the various age levels. As indicated in Table X, the differences between the upper and lower occupational groups for the mean length of response proved to be statistically significant in all but the eighteen-months-old group, in which the number of comprehensible responses involved was much smaller than in any of the other groups.

TABLE X

THE SIGNIFICANCE OF THE DIFFERENCES BETWEEN THE MEAN LENGTHS
OF RESPONSE IN THE UPPER AND LOWER OCCUPATIONAL GROUPS

CA	MEAN FOR OCCUPATIONAL GROUPS		D	$\dfrac{D}{SD_{diff.}}$
	Upper Half	Lower Half		
18	1.61	1.33	.28	1.11
24 and 30	3.01	2.34	.67	2.51
36 and 42	5.38	3.28	2.10	10.55
48 and 54	4.84	4.20	.64	5.66

MENTAL AGE

The mean length of sentence has been considered also in relation to mental age. The material on mental age reported in this study has three sources of error. The first is the error in the standardization of the Kuhlmann scale, which was brought out by the Goodenough [27] restandardization, in which it is shown that the Kuhlmann test is too easy at all the ages involved in the study and particularly at the four-year level. It is in error 0.9 of a month of mental age at year two, 0.8 of a month at year three, and 4.7 months at year four. A correction could be made for these discrepancies, but it was not thought worth while in view of the second source of error involved in this material.

The second respect in which this material is in error is that the mental tests were not given on the same date on which the observations of this experiment were made. Most of them were given before the experiment was conducted, and many of them over a year before. The mental ages at the time of the observations on language were calculated by multiplying the CA by the IQ. This procedure assumes the constancy of the IQ and accurate standardization of the test itself. If the correction for the inaccuracies of the scale were made, it would have to be done by using the chronological age at which the test was given and not the age at which the child was classified in this study.

Thirdly, many of the children in this investigation had had more than one intelligence test, and although the second test

Fig.4

Mean Length of Response by M A and Sex

is somewhat more reliable than the first (Goodenough [27]), the first test was used for all children because only one test record was available for some of the subjects. However, these inaccuracies are not peculiar to this investigation but are practically inherent in the test method as it is used today and hold true for nearly all work that presents material on mental age. Although the chronological age groups are discrete because of the way in which the subjects were chosen with respect to age, it was not possible to have the mental age groups similarly discrete. While the mental age series is really continuous, it has been thrown into class intervals of six months for tabulation, and for purposes of rough comparison with the chronological age groups.

The mean number of words per response for each mental age group is shown in Fig. 4. It will be seen that in spite of this grouping according to mental age, the sex differences still persist in favor of the girls. The mean length of response shows the same sort of curve when considered in relation to mental age that it does when plotted against chronological age until fifty-four months, when it practically reaches a maximum and shows very little increment with increase in mental age beyond the point of maximum chronological age. This is interesting in view of the previously mentioned findings of Nice [50] and Doran.[20]

The differences that were indicated above between the various occupational groups in the mean length of sentence might be due to the different intelligence levels that each occupational group represents. In order to test this hypothesis, the mean length of response has been considered in relation to paternal occupation and to mental age as shown in Fig. 5.*

* Several gaps occurred in the data for Figs. 4 and 5. In Fig. 4, there were no boys who fell in the two highest mental age groups. In Fig. 5, there were no members of Occupational Group I at the four mental age levels 12 and 18, 36 and 42, 60 and 66, and 72 and 78 months. No members of Group II belonged at mental age level 60 and 66 months, and there were no members of the IV, V, or VI occupational groups at the highest mental age level. The figures are drawn as closely as possible in accordance with the data, but where gaps occurred, straight lines have been drawn between the two given plotting points.

It will be seen here that while the differences are not as consistent as in the chronological age table, there is still a

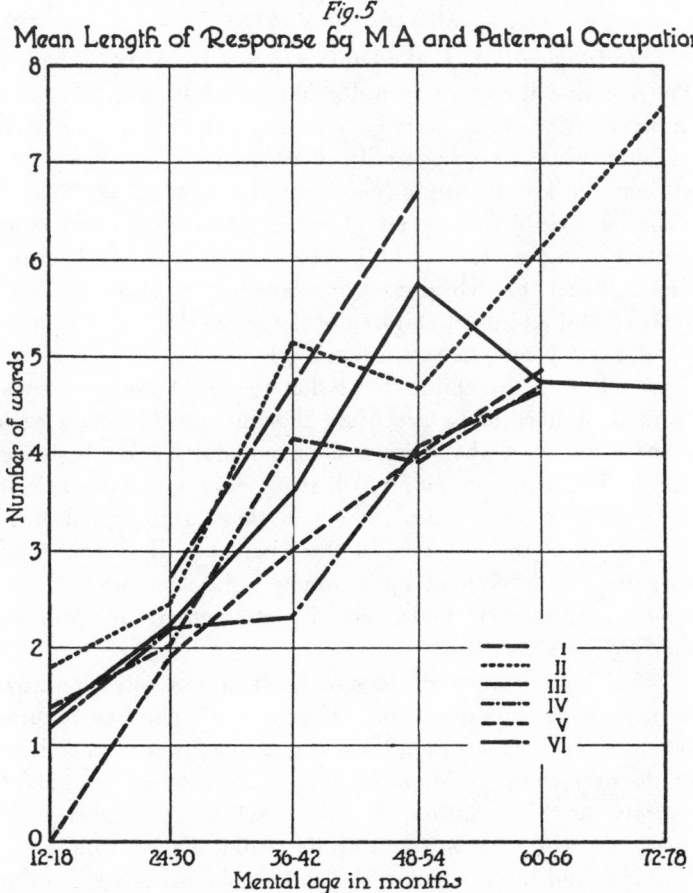

Fig.5

Mean Length of Response by M A and Paternal Occupation

tendency for the upper occupational groups to remain superior to the lower groups when mental age is constant. Thus, mental age is probably a factor that enters into the occupational group differences to some extent, but it certainly is not the only factor that is operative.

AGE OF ASSOCIATES

We frequently hear the belief expressed popularly, and in the scientific literature as well, that the child who associates entirely with · adults, or who spends most of his time with children who are considerably older than he, is usually precocious in his linguistic development. The Gales [24] said, "The later children have an advantage in learning much from contact with the older child." This statement is based on the fact that their first child used only one-half as many words as their second and third children at the same age. On the other hand, some people maintain that adults' conversation is so far removed from the child's level that the child can gain little from it, and children are often thought to understand each other much better than they understand adults. One basis for this is the frequency with which twins develop a language of their own, a development which is thought to retard their acquisition of the language of their parents. Hall [30] says, in speaking of children of approximately the same age, "Their noises are too well understood by each other, the younger holding the older back."

This investigation afforded a good opportunity to throw some light on this question. Of course, all children of preschool age associate with adults, but an attempt was made here to discover those children who associate with adults almost entirely, to the exclusion of child playmates. In nearly all cases the mother was asked if the child played with other children, and if so, whether the child's playmates were much older, about the same age, or younger than he. Children who were in day nurseries or in institutions were considered as associating with children about their own ages. In a large proportion of the cases, this information could be obtained first hand, since the other children in the family were frequently seen during some part of the home visit, or the child was called in from play with the children in the neighborhood for the observation.

The subjects of this experiment were all placed in three arbitrary groups on the basis of the ages of their associates. Group 1 includes all children who spend most of their time with associates over twelve years of age. Group 2 includes children who, in addition to association with adults, also associate with children who are more than two years older than they. Group 3 includes all children who, in addition to association with adults, also associate with children their own ages or younger; that is, with children who are not more than two years older than they.

These three groups were then considered with respect to the mean length of sentence. Each child was given a percentile rank within his own age level, on the basis of his mean length of response. Then the median percentile rank for each of the above groups was computed. The results of this analysis were as follows: For twenty-seven children whose associates were chiefly adults, the median percentile rank for length of response was 70; for seventy children who associated with older children, 42.5; and for forty-three who associated with children their own ages and younger, 52.5.

Thus we see that those who associate with adults only seem to have a decided advantage in the length of sentence over those who associate with children. The figures for the other two groups, however, are the reverse of the expectations. In order to determine if this difference was due to a pre ponderance of either sex in either of these two groups that might account for the figures, the number of boys and the number of girls in each group was tabulated. It was found that the sexes were equally represented in each of these groups, so that a sex difference in the mean length of response cannot account for the differences in the median percentile ranks for these age-of-associates groups.

The differences between the occupational groups represent another factor that might be operative in bringing about this result. The tabulation of the number of children in the various occupational groups in each of the above groups revealed the following facts: Of the 27 children who associated chiefly with adults, 13 were from the upper social classes, and 14 were from the lower social classes. Of the 43 children who associated with the children their own ages and younger, 22 belonged to the upper occupational groups, while 21 belonged to the lower occupational groups. Of the 70 children who associated with older children, only 30 were from the upper half, while 40 were from the lower half of the occupational scale. Thus, the upper and lower occupational groups are equally represented in Groups 1 and 3, while there is a marked excess of the members of the lower occupational groups in Group 2 which, no doubt, accounts for the lower median percentile rank of this group of children who associate with older children. In this case we have operating the factor that large families are more numerous in the lower occupational groups, and it is in large families that we most frequently find the preschool child associating with older children. Here again, we have the factor of intelligence operating in the same way as it did in previous instances. The mean IQ for Group 1 equals 113, for Group 2, 106, and for Group 3, 107. There are so many factors involved in the situation and these are so intimately related to each other, that it is difficult to isolate any one of them as the sole factor that brings about such a result. The clear superiority of the children who associate chiefly with adults certainly is not due either to the sex differences, or to the occupational group differences. It does seem to be related to intelligence, but probably the important factor that functions here is that the situation in which the data were collected was that of talking to an adult which, no doubt, placed those who were accustomed to associating chiefly with adults at a decided advantage.

BILINGUALISM

The factor of bilingualism is another problem about which there has been a great deal of speculation, but about which few facts are known. Since 10 per cent of the children in this study heard a foreign language in the home, it seemed advisable to study them in more detail. The numbers involved here are too few to allow any conclusions to be drawn, but the tendencies found are suggestive and indicate some other problems that might be attacked by a method similar to that of the present study.

TABLE XI

MEDIAN PERCENTILE RANK
ACCORDING TO FOREIGN LANGUAGE HEARD AND PATERNAL OCCUPATION

LANGUAGE	N	OCCUPATIONAL GROUP	MEDIAN PERCENTILE
Polish	6	5 in VI, 1 in V	25
Italian	1	VI	5
Slovak	1	VI	5
German	2	II	63
Finnish	1	VI	40
Swedish	1	IV	45
Norwegian	1	I	100
Esperanto	1	I	100

The median percentile rank on the basis of the mean length of response for the 14 children who heard a foreign language in the home was 40. This is only slightly below the central tendency of the group as a whole and is especially surprising when we consider that 9 were boys, and only 5 were girls. Again this result is surprising when we note the tabulation of these cases according to paternal occupation as 2 belonged in Occupational Group I, 2 in Group II, none in Group III, 1 in Group IV, 1 in Group V, and 8 were members of Group VI. This indicates that it is the extreme groups that hear a foreign language, and that over half of the occurrence of bilingualism is in the sixth occupational group. Table XI shows the median percentile rank according to the language heard.

Thus, it appears that in spite of a predominance of boys and a great overweighting of the lower occupational groups, bilingualism does not seem to be a serious handicap in linguistic development as measured by the mean length of response. However, this does not mean that it is not a handicap to proper pronunciation and construction. All we can conclude from these meager data is that the hearing of a foreign language in the home does not seem to be a handicap in linguistic development as it is measured by the mean length of response, which, when applied to larger groups, has proved a very reliable index.

MEAN LENGTHS OF RESPONSES IN ORDER OF OCCURRENCE

In order to determine the extent to which shyness entered into the experimental situation, the mean lengths of the first ten responses, of the second ten, of the third ten, etc., were calculated. It was expected that shyness would exhibit itself by a tendency to shorter responses, and that any tendency for an initial shyness to be overcome during the period of observation would be indicated by this series of means for the responses taken in groups of ten, in the order in which they were recorded. The figures for this analysis for all age levels together are shown in Table XII.

It will be seen from this table that the children's responses tended to be somewhat shorter at first, but that there is little change in the mean length after the first ten or twenty responses. The mean for the initial responses for the girls is relatively lower than it is for the boys, and the maximum level is reached more slowly by them than it is by the boys. This result would seem to indicate greater shyness among the girls of the group, as is evidenced by shorter verbal responses.

TABLE XII

MEAN LENGTHS OF RESPONSES IN ORDER OF OCCURRENCE

	1ST TEN	2ND TEN	3RD TEN	4TH TEN	5TH TEN
Boys	2.88	3.24	3.23	3.27	3.26
Girls	2.76	3.33	3.53	3.39	3.38
All	2.82	3.29	3.34	3.32	3.35

TIME REQUIRED TO OBTAIN FIFTY RESPONSES

The length of time that was required to secure fifty responses from each child was recorded at the time of observation. This varied greatly with the individual child, as the range for the length of the observation period was from seven to fifty minutes. The mean length of time for recording for each age level and by sex is shown in Table XIII.

It will be noted that the mean time required for observation changed very little with chronological age. This is due to the fact that while the younger children say very little and have long intervals between their responses, the older children talk much more, use longer sentences (which take longer to record), and give more elicited responses. These factors seem to operate to balance each other, so that the length of the observation remains fairly constant at the various age levels, although there is a slight tendency, which is more marked among the boys, for the older children to have a shorter observation period. No consistent sex difference appears in this series of figures, which may mean no sex difference in shyness if the measure of the length of time required to obtain fifty responses is considered an index of shyness. The time required to secure fifty responses gave a correlation of —.203 with the total number of words used by each child and a correlation of +.126 with the percentage of elicited responses for each child.

TABLE XIII

MEAN TIME REQUIRED TO OBTAIN FIFTY RESPONSES
BY CA AND SEX

CA	BOYS	GIRLS	ALL
18	23.77	22.45	22.70
24	21.50	21.50	21.50
30	17.50	20.75	19.45
36	18.63	17.44	18.10
42	16.41	17.62	16.90
48	18.22	19.54	18.95
54	16.54	19.66	17.30

SUMMARY

1. The mean percentage of comprehensible responses increases rapidly with increase in chronological age and the percentage is much larger for the girls than for the boys at each age level.

2. The mean was found to be the most reliable measure of the length of response.

3. The mean length of response shows a steady increase with chronological age, which is most rapid between eighteen and forty-two months.

4. A small but consistent sex difference in favor of the girls is found for the mean length of response.

5. The length of response shows marked differences from

one occupational group to the other, each group maintaining its proper relative position quite consistently.

6. When considered in relation to mental age, the mean length of response shows the same type of curve as when it is considered in relation to chronological age.

7. The sex differences still persist in spite of the mental age grouping.

8. Children who associate chiefly with adults show a much greater mean length of response than do those who associate with children.

9. The hearing of a foreign language in the home does not seem to be a serious handicap to linguistic development as measured by the mean length of response.

10. The first ten responses recorded average lower than the succeeding groups of ten responses. This may indicate an overcoming of shyness during the observation.

11. The mean time required to obtain fifty responses shows very little change with chronological age.

CHAPTER IV

FUNCTIONAL ANALYSIS

Another aspect of the child's language which is interesting to consider, and which has heretofore received very little attention from investigators, is the function of the response in relation to the child's environment. For what purpose does the child talk? What needs does he satisfy by the use of verbal responses? In what situations are verbal responses brought forth, what kinds of responses are used in these various situations, and what changes do these responses show as the child grows older? These are some of the questions upon which this analysis is intended to throw some light. It is an attempt to give a total picture of the child's language and its development from the functional point of view, as it is evidenced in the samplings obtained in this experiment. As Claparède says in his preface to Piaget's study,[56] "The problem of child mentality has been thought of as one of quantity, M. Piaget has restated it as a problem of quality." Certainly there is another, and much broader aspect of the child's linguistic development, in addition to that which was discussed in the previous chapter. Piaget [56] seems to be interested in this functional aspect chiefly as it reveals the child's thought processes and his logic.

Snyder [62] has approached this functional problem by modifying the old grammatical classification of sentences and by making subheads and variations of several groups. Smith [61] has used the Snyder [62] classification with some modifications. All find these categories arbitrary and quite unsatisfactory when applied to the speech of the child. For the functional analysis of this study, therefore, the classification of Piaget,[56] with modifications as outlined in Chapter II, has been adopted.

CHRONOLOGICAL AGE

The first and most interesting phase of an analysis such as this is its total composition at any time, and the changes that appear in it with increase in chronological age. The number of children considered in this study is small for statistical considerations, and especially so when we have to consider each age group separately. Then, when the fifty responses of each child are scattered over ten or twelve different categories, it can hardly be expected that differences will be found from one age level to another that would be considered statistically significant. The data are really too meager to warrant such over-refinement of the method. However, as will be pointed out, the trends indicated are consistent through seven age levels, for the sexes separately, and when considered in relation to certain other factors; and, hence, probably are significant, even though they would not measure up to the usual standard of statistical significance. Smith,[61] who has attempted to apply the statistical measures of significance of differences to her material, says:

Classification of sentences into types according to use gives no significant increase or decrease in any one type in the percentage used from year to year or from the youngest group to the oldest group, although as the child grows older there seems to be a possible trend towards increase in the number of questions asked and towards a decrease in the number of exclamatory sentences. On the other hand, there are significant differences between the percentages when one type of sentence is compared with another. Thus there are more declarative sentences, at all ages, than any other type. Also the proportion of imperative sentences, including variations, is probably significantly greater than the proportion of questions at two, three, and four years. The only further significant difference seems to be the greater percentage of imperative sentences than "Yes" and "No" only.

In the present analysis the percentage of each item was found for each child, and the mean percentages according to age and sex groups are presented in the tables and diagrams in this chapter.

Since only the comprehensible responses could be scored according to this analysis, the incomprehensible responses are included as a separate category in order to give a picture of the total number of responses obtained. Perhaps Piaget [56] would have included these incomprehensible responses under one type of egocentric responses, particularly under echolalia, but the children whom he observed were six and seven years old, and had little or no speech that was incomprehensible. Probably all the incomprehensible responses that he recorded were mere voice-play for those children. With these younger subjects, however, the inflections with which the incomprehensible responses were uttered would lead one to believe that in many cases, the responses were highly social and intended to convey meaning to the hearer. It seems that in such cases, it is better to leave the incomprehensible responses as a separate group to be studied by a different technique and not to try to score such responses according to the functional categories.

Egocentric responses, it will be noted (Table XIV and Fig. 6), are a very small proportion of the total number of responses at all age levels. This is contrary to the findings of Piaget,[56] who says that the two children whom he studied, who were six and one-half years of age, had an egocentric language that amounted to nearly half of their total spontaneous speech. The discrepancy here may be due to a number of factors. The primary one seems to be the different situations in which the children were observed. His observations were made during free-play periods with other children in the school at the Institute Rousseau. Frequently children were observed while they were playing alone, or if in the presence of other children, while they were not engaged in cooperative play. They were merely accompanying

TABLE XIV

Mean Per Cent Each Item of the Functional Analysis by CA and Sex

CA	Sex	Ego-Cent.	Adapt. Inform.	Criti-cism	Emot. Resp.	Ques-tions	An-swers	Social Phrase	Dram. Imit.
18	B	.4	6.5	0.0	2.9	.4	0.0	2.7	.9
	G	1.1	23.4	0.0	4.5	4.7	1.4	1.8	.4
	All	.8	15.8	0.0	3.8	2.8	.1	2.2	.6
24	B	5.0	15.8	0.0	8.9	5.3	10.0	1.3	1.3
	G	3.2	30.4	.3	12.4	10.4	17.2	1.0	1.0
	All	3.9	24.6	.2	11.0	8.4	10.0	1.1	1.1
30	B	5.3	52.5	.8	16.8	4.5	9.0	1.8	1.5
	G	2.5	50.7	2.0	9.8	2.2	16.0	2.3	.7
	All	3.6	51.4	1.5	12.6	3.1	13.0	2.1	1.0
36	B	3.5	47.6	.4	8.7	10.9	16.0	0.0	1.6
	G	3.3	52.0	.4	9.1	14.3	20.0	.7	0.0
	All	3.4	49.6	.4	8.9	12.5	18.0	.3	.9
42	B	7.2	47.0	.3	9.3	10.6	19.0	.3	.7
	G	.5	58.8	0.0	9.0	8.0	22.0	.8	2.8
	All	4.6	52.2	.2	9.2	9.6	20.0	.5	1.5
48	B	1.6	38.8	1.6	9.0	12.8	33.0	.2	2.0
	G	1.1	50.7	.6	4.3	11.5	29.0	0.0	1.1
	All	1.3	45.3	1.0	6.5	12.1	31.0	.1	1.5
54	B	1.8	59.0	.9	5.6	10.1	22.0	.9	1.3
	G	2.7	49.1	.4	7.3	5.8	32.0	1.3	2.0
	All	2.2	54.6	.7	6.4	8.2	26.0	1.1	1.6

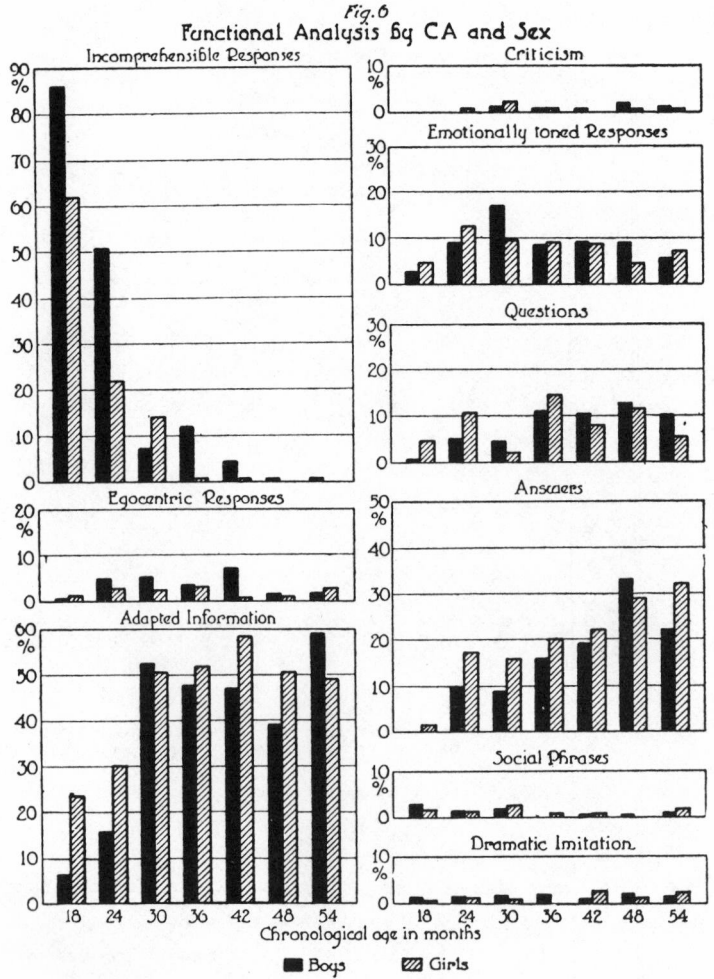

Fig. 6
Functional Analysis by CA and Sex

their actions with words and verbalizing about the activity of the moment regardless of an audience. This sort of situation, which was frequent in the observations of both Piaget [56] and Smith,[61] seldom occurred in the present study. The presence of a stranger in the home, who displayed a set of new toys, was very conducive to socialized speech. The factor of individual differences is probably of greatest importance in this category, for there were a few extreme cases in this study, of children who disregarded the experimenter during the greater part of the observations and hence had an exceptionally high percentage of egocentric responses. When only two children were used, as in the Piaget [56] study, it is possible that the high degree of egocentricity found was largely because of a peculiarity in the individual children. In fact, Piaget [56] says of one of the children whom he studied, "Lev is a little fellow who is very much wrapped up in himself. He is always telling every one else what he is doing at the moment."

While the classification has proved very reliable, it is possible that the general bias of the scorer in favor of regarding most responses as egocentric if they are not definitely socialized, i.e., addressed to a particular person, might tend to skew the whole scoring system towards a larger proportion of egocentric responses. Piaget [56] has called our attention to a very important, and heretofore unrecognized, aspect of language, which is particularly important in the primitive language of the child; but in so doing, i.e., in looking for speech that is mere talking for the pleasure of talking and not for the purpose of communicating thought, he has tended to magnify its importance and has overemphasized it. This overemphasis of a new point of view frequently occurs and it is probably well that it should be so, in order to attract the attention that it deserves.

Piaget,[56] in attempting to bring out the importance of speech that does not have the communication of thought as its sole function, says that it is futile to attempt to reduce the functions of language to one—that of communicating thought. We must realize, however, that while some speech does not have the purely social function of communicating thought to others, this is one of the primary uses of language and its most frequent use by the adult. If we are to judge the child's degree of language development by the degree to which he approximates adult language, why not approach the material from the point of view of the criterion, i.e., from the point of view of the mature form towards which it is developing, and consider any responses that might be social on the part of the child as socialized responses if they are not definitely egocentric?

Piaget [56] seems to have approached the data from the opposite point of view, namely, that a response is definitely egocentric unless it is clearly socialized. A child may talk about himself, and yet communicate ideas with the purpose of influencing his hearer. After giving some examples of egocentric speech, Piaget [56] says,

> The whole of this monologue has no further aim than to accompany the action as it takes place. . . . . Pie would like to inform someone about his plans (sentences 55 and 57). But in spite of this the monologue runs on uninterrupted as though Pie were alone in the room. Speech in this case functions only as a stimulus, and in no wise as a means of communication. . . . . [In the examples referred to], Pie takes his arithmetic copy-book and turns the pages: "1, 2, . . . 3, 4, 5, 6, 7 . . . 8 . . . 8888 and 8 . . . 9. Number 9, number 9, number 9 (singing) I want number 9." (This is the number he is going to represent by a drawing.) . . . . [Sentence 55] (Mlle. L. passes by his table without saying anything.) "Look, teacher, 9, 9, 9 . . . number 9." . . . . [Sentence 57] (to Ez as he passes): "I'm doing 9, I am—. . . . ." (Ez) "What are you going to do?"—"Little rounds."

It seems that sentence 55 is a socialized response, in that the teacher is addressed and the child attempts to tell her something. Sentence 57, although the child is talking about himself, is attracting the attention of the other child and communicating an idea to him which brings about a dialogue in the form of a question asked by the second child. This question is then answered by Pie. We can hardly admit that all of these responses are egocentric. Piaget [56] himself admits their social character when he says, as mentioned above, "Pie would like to inform someone about his plans." Moreover, since the child is not alone, how does he know that "the monologue runs on as though Pie were alone in the room," and how does he know that "if he were alone, his remarks would be substantially the same"? It seems that in looking for this newly recognized aspect of language, the author has tended to fall into the error that he admits in his foreword, "that an experiment is always influenced by the hypothesis which occasioned it."

Justification of the discrepancy between the results of the present study and those of the Piaget [56] study is found, however, in the reliability tests (see Chapter II) in which the four scorers, all using Piaget's [56] own definitions, agreed in finding very little speech which they classed as egocentric. This would tend to indicate that the difference is not due to a subjective factor of scoring but to a difference in the material, which probably can be accounted for by a difference in the conditions under which the data were collected. It is possible that the true proportion of egocentric speech in the younger subjects has been obscured in the present study by the separation of the incomprehensible responses, a large proportion of which (just what proportion it is impossible to determine from this material) is probably egocentric in character. Any or all of the above-mentioned factors may have contributed in bringing about the difference in the results of the two studies. Egocentric responses appear in such small numbers all through that they show no trends with age, and no noticeable sex differences. Because of this large difference in the results of the two studies, it is hardly possible to compare the percentages on the other items, since they are on a relative basis.

Adapted information is the largest single group of socialized speech. Its absolute increase with age is marked, and, as will be seen from Fig. 6, it increases from about 5 or 10 per cent at eighteen' months to about 50 per cent by fifty-four months, so that it becomes, by far, the major proportion of the conversation of the older children of this group.

Criticism is a very small group that does not appear at all in the eighteen-months-old subjects. It seems to be related more to individual personality traits and shows no tendency to change with age or sex.

The third type of socialized speech, which has been called emotionally toned responses, shows some very interesting changes with increase in chronological age. The relationship can best be seen in Table XV and in Fig. 7. It is clear that this group of wishes, requests, commands, and the like makes up a very large part of the comprehensible speech of the young child, and that it becomes relatively less important as the child grows older. It seems that the child first uses comprehensible language in situations and about things that have a decided emotional tone. This corroborates previous findings reported in the literature, for most investigators report a large proportion of imperative sentences in the younger children, and a decrease in them with advance in age. Piaget [56] points out that Janet "considered that the earliest words are derived from cries with which animals and even savages accompany their action . . . . threats, cries of anger in the fight, etc. . . . . Hence the earliest words of all, which are words of command." Yerkes and Learned [78] found similar facts for the utterances of the young chimpanzees that they studied. There were characteristic vocalizations made for different situations, which were more in the nature of emotional expression than designations for objects per se.

TABLE XV

Mean Per Cent Each Item of the Functional Analysis by CA and Sex
(Based on Comprehensible Responses Only)

CA	Sex	Ego-Cent.	Adapt. Inform.	Criti-cism	Emot. Resp.	Ques-tions	An-swers	Social Phrase	Dram. Imit.
18	B	3.1	46.1	0.0	20.6	3.1	0.0	19.1	6.4
	G	2.9	61.5	0.0	12.0	12.5	3.7	4.8	1.0
	All	3.1	60.6	0.0	14.6	10.8	.3	8.5	2.3
24	B	10.2	32.1	0.0	18.1	10.7	20.4	2.6	2.6
	G	4.1	38.6	.4	15.9	13.4	22.0	1.3	1.3
	All	6.5	40.8	.3	18.3	13.9	16.6	1.9	1.7
30	B	5.7	56.5	.8	18.0	4.8	9.7	1.9	1.6
	G	2.9	58.9	2.3	11.4	3.6	18.6	2.7	.8
	All	4.0	57.7	1.7	14.2	3.5	14.6	2.4	1.1
36	B	4.0	54.1	.4	9.9	12.4	18.2	0.0	1.9
	G	3.3	52.0	.4	9.1	14.3	20.0	.7	0.0
	All	3.6	50.9	.4	9.4	13.2	19.1	.3	1.0
42	B	7.7	49.2	.4	9.8	11.1	19.9	.4	.7
	G	.5	58.8	0.0	9.0	8.0	22.0	.8	2.8
	All	4.7	53.2	.2	9.4	9.7	20.4	.5	1.5
48	B	1.6	38.8	1.6	9.0	12.8	33.0	.2	2.0
	G	1.1	50.6	.6	4.3	11.5	29.0	0.0	1.1
	All	1.3	45.2	1.0	6.5	12.1	31.0	.1	1.5
54	B	1.8	59.0	.9	5.6	10.1	22.0	.9	1.3
	G	2.7	49.1	.4	7.3	5.8	32.0	1.3	2.0
	All	2.2	54.6	.7	6.4	8.2	26.0	1.1	1.6

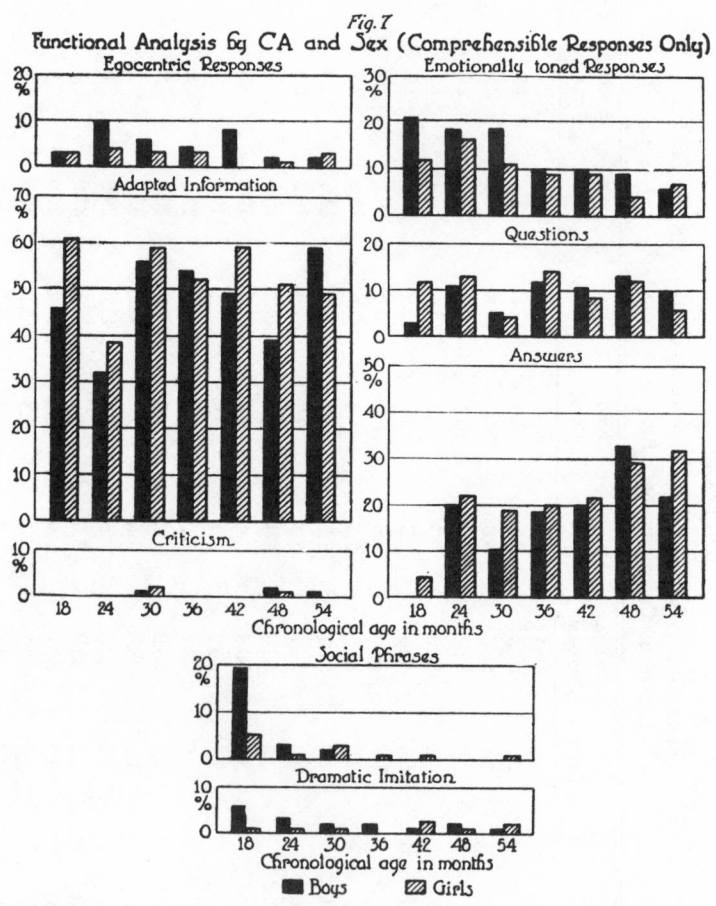

Fig. 7
Functional Analysis by CA and Sex (Comprehensible Responses Only)

Questions, when considered in relation to the total number of responses as in Table XIV and Fig. 6, increase with advance in chronological age most rapidly at the younger age levels. However, when we consider them in relation to the comprehensible responses only (Table XV and Fig. 7), they are relatively quite important at the lower age levels and maintain their position consistently throughout the other groups. This result is interesting in connection with personality traits, in view of the fact that Marston [42] reports that the number of questions the child asked about the exhibits in a museum was roughly indicative of his degree of extroversion.

Answers are not found at all among the boys of eighteen months, but thereafter increase markedly with chronological age, so that by the ages of forty-eight and fifty-four months they represent between one-fourth and one-third of the total number of responses.

Social phrases are about 3 per cent of the total number of responses, and about 19 per cent of the number of comprehensible responses of the boys eighteen months of age. They decrease in relative importance and occupy a comparatively insignificant place throughout the upper ages.

Dramatic imitation is also a small group that shows no definite tendency in relation to chronological age. It seems to be related more to personality factors of the individual children, to their habits of play, and to chance factors in the situation.

To summarize then the findings with regard to the functional analysis in relation to chronological age, we may say that the categories that increase markedly with age are: adapted information, questions, and answers. Emotionally toned responses show a decrease in relative importance with increase in chronological age.

SEX DIFFERENCES

As will be seen from the diagrams that have been under consideration in the preceding paragraphs, there is a consistent difference in the items that show trends with increase in chronological age in favor of the more rapid development of these functions among the girls. The incomprehensible responses, as noted before, are much less numerous among the girls of eighteen months, only 62 per cent as compared with 86 per cent for the boys. This difference persists, with the exception of a slight reversal at thirty months, which is due, no doubt, to the few highly selected boys at this age, and these incomprehensible responses disappear earlier among the girls than they do among the boys.

Egocentric responses are a very small proportion of the responses in both sexes and show no differences that are consistently in favor of either sex.

Adapted information as a single group constitutes 6 per cent of the total number of responses among the boys at eighteen months, and 23 per cent among the girls of the same age. The superiority of the girls in the amount of this type of speech, which later constitutes one-half of the conversation of older children, is indicated throughout; although the boys tend to equal them in the higher age levels. It seems as if the girls have a more rapid rise in the learning curve, indicating that they go through the developmental cycle more rapidly than do the boys, but both arrive eventually at approximately the same level.

Emotionally toned responses show a decrease in relative importance with increase in chronological age. From Table XV and Fig. 7 we see that of the comprehensible responses, the emotionally toned responses constitute only about half as large a proportion among the girls at eighteen months as among the boys. The difference becomes smaller but persists at the next two age levels, indicating a more rapid falling off of this type of response among the girls, until the two sexes equal each other at a fairly stable level in the upper age groups.

Questions show no differences between the sexes that are consistent at all ages.

Answers, as noted above, show a steady increase with age and are a larger proportion among the girls at six of the seven age levels. They are not found at all among the boys of eighteen months, whereas they form 1.4 per cent of the total number of responses, and 3.7 per cent of the comprehensible responses of the girls at that age. This group includes all the elicited responses, and if the percentage of elicited

TABLE XVI

MEAN PER CENT EACH TYPE OF ADAPTED INFORMATION
BY CA AND SEX

CA	SEX	NAMING	IMMED. SIT.	ASSOC. SIT.	IRREL.
18	B	86.2	13.8	.0	.0
	G	88.4	10.1	1.5	.0
24	B	69.8	30.2	.0	.0
	G	54.0	35.6	9.3	1.1
30	B	45.7	34.8	19.5	.0
	G	49.7	30.6	16.4	3.3
36	B	41.4	33.4	22.5	2.7
	G	32.1	49.1	16.9	3.8
42	B	40.6	40.4	17.9	1.1
	G	36.6	37.9	24.3	1.3
48	B	24.1	59.9	11.5	4.6
	G	25.2	37.2	32.5	5.0
54	B	30.8	40.8	27.1	1.2
	G	18.6	48.0	30.8	2.7

responses is any index of shyness, this may mean greater shyness on the part of the girls.

The other two items of this functional classification, namely, social phrases and dramatic imitation, are too small in number to allow any sex differences to appear. Their occurrence seems to be a matter of personality traits of the individual children.

ADAPTED INFORMATION

In the preceding section, adapted information was considered as one whole category. Let us now analyze it in more detail to note the changes that occur in the four subdivisions of this group. In Table XVI and Fig. 8, adapted information

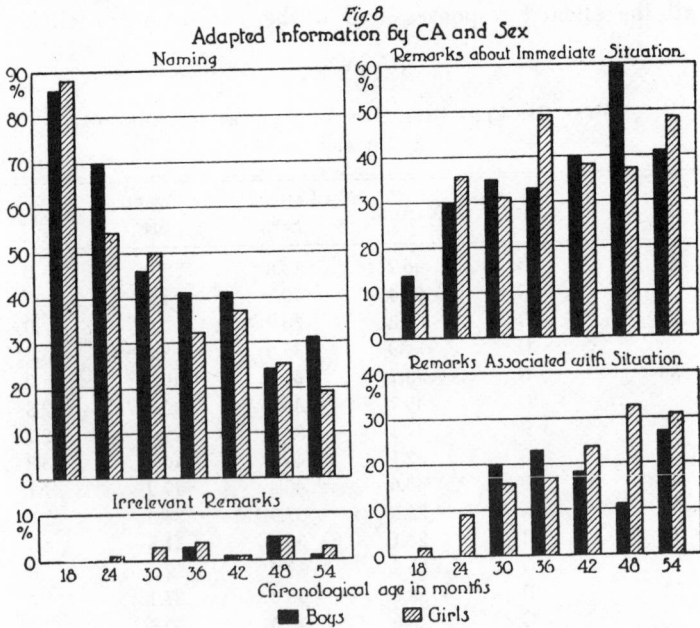

Fig. 8
Adapted Information by CA and Sex

is considered as 100 per cent, and the proportion that each subdivision is of the whole is indicated. It is clear that naming constitutes by far the major portion of the adapted information group among the younger children. Of the total number of responses it equals 5.6 per cent among the boys of eighteen months and 20.6 per cent among the girls of the same age.

These proportions equal 86.2 per cent and 88.4 per

cent, respectively, of the total number of responses classed as adapted information. There is a steady decrease in the proportion of naming from age to age, until at fifty-four months it equals 18 per cent of the total number of responses of the boys and 9 per cent of the total number of responses of the girls. The dropping off of this more primitive type of response seems to occur first among the girls, although the difference is not marked.

Many writers in the literature report a naming stage in the child's linguistic development. Koffka [37] gives an interesting account of this problem of the "name question." He says that it is a typical phenomenon and is the factor upon which progress in speech development is chiefly based, and that in the single-word stage, the word has a wish or affective character. "The word frees itself from this wish-affective relation and enters into a new relation with things." In order for this to occur, "thing configurations" must first be present. "The configuration of the thing concept should have a core or center to which the members adhere in a definite manner; i.e., a thing has its attributes, but the peculiar kind of cohesion is the essential thing. The word enters into the thing pattern and becomes an attribute of the thing and yet a peculiar attribute in that anything may possess it."

The existence of this naming stage is confirmed by the findings of most investigators, as well as by those of the word analysis of the present study. These results indicate a rapid acquisition of nouns in this early stage, before the appearance of many of the other parts of speech. As indicated in the introductory chapter, however, these single-word responses, which we class as mere naming, frequently stand for whole sentences and often express commands, wishes, and other forms of expression; and many of the words that we class as nouns have other than the substantive function.

Remarks about the immediate situation are the next most

frequent type of adapted information at all age levels. They increase considerably in relative amount from eighteen to twenty-four months, and maintain a fairly constant relationship thereafter. No sex difference is apparent for this group of responses.

TABLE XVII

MEAN PER CENT MAIN ITEMS OF THE FUNCTIONAL ANALYSIS
BY CA AND PATERNAL OCCUPATION

CA	OCCUP. GROUP	EGO-CENT.	ADAPT. INFORM.	CRITI-CISM	EMOT. RESP.	QUES-TIONS	AN-SWERS
18	I, II, III,	1.0	19.1	.01	5.0	3.4	1.6
	IV, V, VI,	.6	12.4	.01	2.6	2.2	.4
24 and 30	I, II, III,	3.6	41.4	.7	12.0	9.9	18.5
	IV, V, VI,	3.8	35.2	1.01	11.6	2.3	10.8
36 and 42	I, II, III,	1.6	54.5	.4	9.3	14.7	17.7
	IV, V, VI,	6.1	47.1	.2	8.6	7.6	18.0
48 and 54	I, II, III,	2.3	53.5	.7	5.1	14.2	24.2
	IV, V, VI,	1.2	48.8	1.0	7.9	6.4	32.3

Remarks associated with the situation seem to be the group of adapted information responses that shows a significant increase with advance in chronological age. It is not represented in the responses of the boys of the two youngest age groups, and it increases with age until it constitutes about 15 per cent of the responses of the children of fifty-four months. This type of response appears first among the girls, and although there is a slight tendency for them to have more of these responses than the boys at the lower age levels, the boys equal them by fifty-four months.

Irrelevant remarks constitute the remainder of the adapted information category. They are few in number at all ages and show no significant trend with age or sex.

PATERNAL OCCUPATION

The largest items of this classification have been studied in relation to paternal occupation in order to see if there are any differences in the make-up of the conversation of the

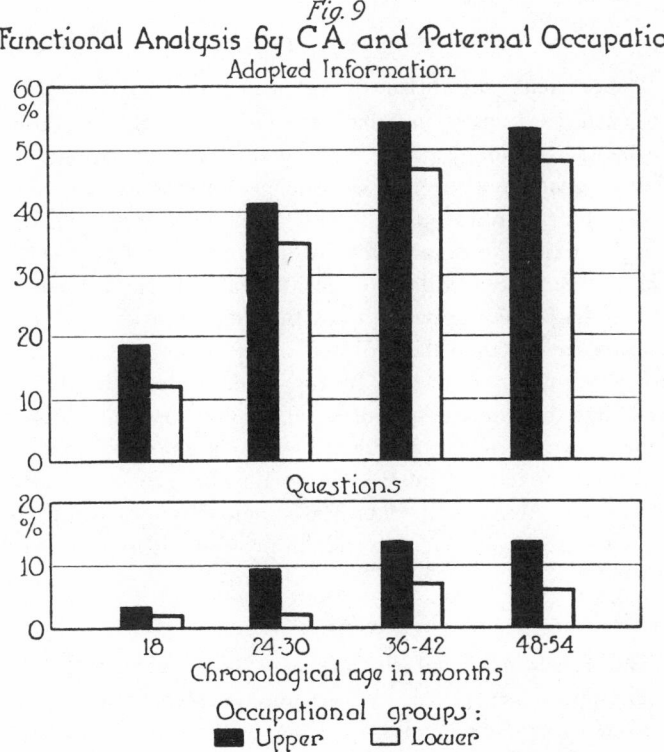

Fig. 9
Functional Analysis by CA and Paternal Occupation
Adapted Information

Questions

Chronological age in months

Occupational groups :
■ Upper   □ Lower

children of the upper and of the lower occupational groups with respect to the different functional uses of speech. As indicated in Table XVII there are two items that show marked differences between the three upper and the three lower occupational groups. They are adapted information and questions, which show very striking differences, as may readily be seen from inspection of Fig. 9. The children in the upper occupational groups have much larger proportions of adapted information and of questions than do those in the lower occupational groups.

AGE OF ASSOCIATES

The various categories of the functional analysis have also been considered in relation to the age of the child's associates. Although there are some large variations, no differences between the age-of-associates groups appear to be consistent or significant. The chief things to note are: first, a large percentage of adapted information found among the eighteen-months-old children who associate almost exclusively with adults. They appear to use this important type of conversation earlier than the children of the same age who associate with other children. In the second place, it may be noted that the younger children who associate with children of their own ages and younger have a larger proportion of emotionally toned responses than do the children of the other two groups. While such data are inconclusive, the tendencies indicated are suggestive and might prove fruitful in further work.

MENTAL AGE

The functional analysis has also been carried through in relation to mental age and, as may be seen from Fig. 10, the same general tendencies appear as with chronological age, but the sex differences are less marked and less consistent. They seem to persist to a slight degree in the per cent of remarks associated with the situation, emotionally toned responses, and answers.

Paternal Occupation.—It might be thought that the differences reported above between the upper and lower occu-

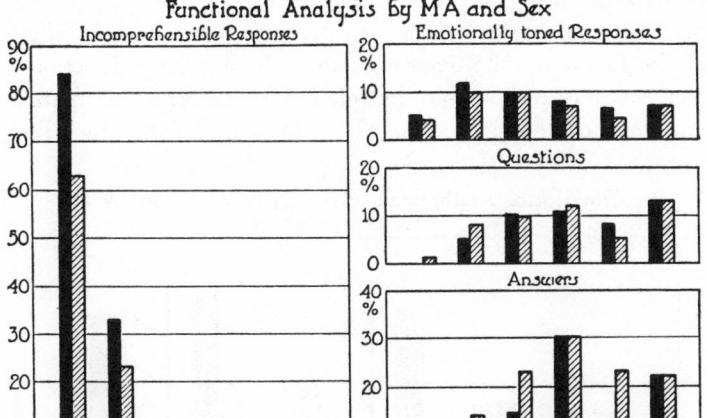

Fig. 10
Functional Analysis by MA and Sex

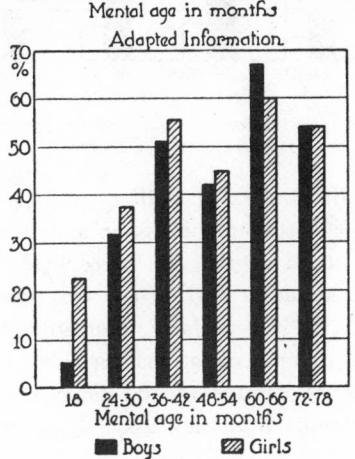

Adapted Information

Mental age in months

■ Boys ▨ Girls

pational groups are due to the different levels of intelligence
that these groups represent. In order to determine the effect
of the factor of intelligence on these findings, the functional
analysis was carried out in relation to paternal occupation
and to mental age. (Fig. 11.) In spite of the fact that

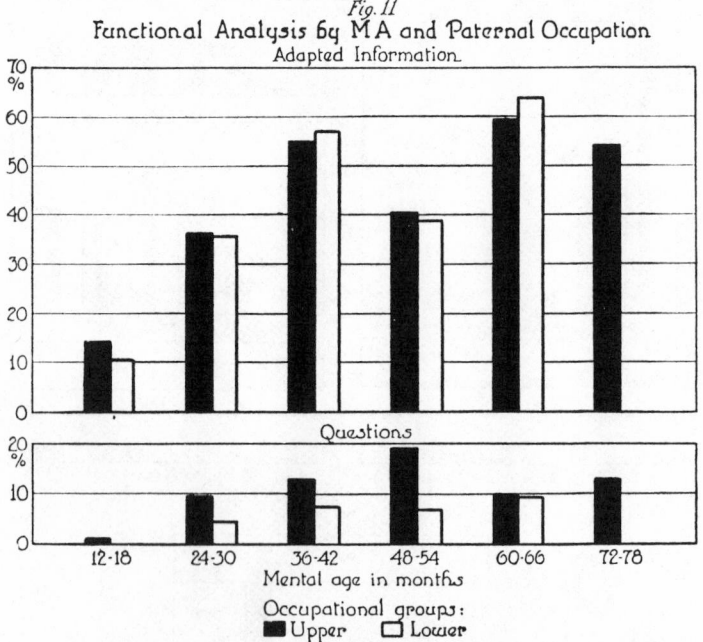

Fig. 11
Functional Analysis by M A and Paternal Occupation
Adapted Information.

mental age is the same for both groups, marked and consistent differences between the upper and lower occupational
groups appear at all ages in the percentage of remarks associated with the situation and in the percentage of questions
that were used. It is especially interesting to note how the
children of the upper occupational groups excel those of the
lower occupational groups of the same mental age in the
number of questions that they ask. It is possible that this

difference is due to their experience in the kind of answers they receive to their questions. Possibly the parents of the children in the upper occupational groups take more pains to answer the children's questions, and the children receive greater satisfaction when they ask questions. In the light of Marston's [42] findings mentioned above, this may mean greater extroversion among the children of the upper occupational groups.

Age of Associates.—The various items of the functional analysis have also been considered in relation to mental age and to the age of associates. These results yield no clear-cut differences among the age-of-associates groups that have the same mental age. The same tendencies, though less distinct, appear here as were noted in the considerations of the age-of-associates groups in relation to chronological age.

SUMMARY

1. The three groups—adapted information, questions, and answers—show marked relative increases with advance in chronological age, while the group of emotionally toned responses shows a relative decrease with advance in chronological age.

2. Small but consistent sex differences, indicating more rapid development of the girls, are shown by the categories that give evidence of developmental trends with chronological age.

3. When adapted information was studied for its various subdivisions, naming was found to decrease with age and to decrease more rapidly among the girls. Remarks associated with the situation show an increase with chronological age, with a tendency for the girls to be superior.

4. Analysis of the functional categories according to paternal occupation reveals a much higher proportion of

adapted information and of questions at all ages among the children of the upper occupational groups.

5. No significant trends appear in the analysis according to the age of associates.

6. Analysis according to mental age groups shows the same tendencies as that according to chronological age, although in some cases they are less marked, and the sex differences are less clear-cut.

7. The same differences between the upper and lower occupational groups appear when mental age is kept constant.

CHAPTER V

CONSTRUCTION ANALYSIS

We have considered the response as a whole from two aspects: according to the length of the response, and according to the function of the response in relation to the situation in which it occurs. There is yet a third important aspect to consider in the study of the linguistic development of the young child—namely, the response as a whole from the point of view of its grammatical structure. This should be studied from the appearance of the single-word sentence, through the beginnings of word combinations such as noun-verb combinations and simple sentences, to the more complex forms of adult language. It is not only important to measure the extent of the child's vocabulary, the increase in the number of different kinds of words, and their proportions in the child's vocabulary from time to time, but also to consider the child's progress in the ability to combine these newly acquired words into various degrees of grammatical complexity. Which grammatical combination appears first, in what sequence do more advanced forms appear, and at what ages do they appear? Questions such as these are attacked in the present analysis.

The classification according to which the responses were scored in this type of approach was described in detail in Chapter II. As was brought out before, adult conversational usage was the criterion of completeness of sentence structure in this analysis. The single-word sentence was scored as one type of complete response because of its adequacy in the situation. Omissions of articles were disregarded. Omission of any essential part of a verbal combination, such as the omission of the auxiliary, was considered an omission of the verb.

In scoring the types of omission for the incomplete sentences, the simplest possible hypothetical completion of the response was used. It is for this reason that no omissions of adjectives, adverbs, or other modifiers appear in the list of omissions, for they are not essential to the simplest form of a complete sentence. The semicomprehensible responses, which were few in number, were scored according to the type of omission wherever possible. Grammatical errors in tense, number, case, gender, and the like were disregarded in this analysis. The emphasis has been chiefly on the complexity of the response as a whole, rather than on correctness of syntax.

ANALYSIS OF SEMICOMPREHENSIBLE AND INCOMPREHENSIBLE RESPONSES

It was, of course, impossible to give construction scores to the semicomprehensible and the incomprehensible responses. A brief analysis of these responses has been conducted, the results of which appear in Table XVIII.

From this analysis we see that the single sound is the predominant type of incomprehensible vocalization among the younger children, and that the series of varied sounds is the next most important type of response, while the repetition of the same sound or babbling is the smallest group of this category. In accordance with the results reported before, the boys have a larger proportion of each type of incomprehensible responses at nearly all age levels, and these responses disappear at an earlier age among the girls. The last column of Table XVIII gives the mean number of syllables per response for all the children of each age level, the sexes taken separately. We note a decrease in the mean number of syllables combined per response with increase in chronological age. This, however, may be somewhat misleading, for it represents means for all the children, many of whom have no responses

TABLE XVIII

MEAN PER CENT EACH TYPE OF INCOMPREHENSIBLE VOCALIZATION

CA	A. SINGLE SOUND		B. REPETITION OF SAME SOUND		C. VARIED SOUNDS		SEMI-COMPREHENSIBLE		AVERAGE NO. SYLLABLES PER INCOMPREHENSIBLE RESPONSE	
	B	G	B	G	B	G	B	G	B	G
18	46.3	21.0	3.2	2.2	34.0	28.8	10.2	9.8	2.7	1.6
24	18.4	9.1	2.3	.2	18.6	8.0	3.8	5.3	1.4	2.0
30	.5	5.2	0.0	.7	1.5	4.5	4.8	3.7	1.6	1.4
36	5.4	0.0	.8	0.0	5.2	.2	1.2	.4	1.6	1.1
42	.3	0.0	0.0	0.0	1.8	0.0	2.3	.3	1.8	.3
48	0.0	.2	0.0	0.0	0.0	0.0	.7	0.0	.6	.9
54	.2	0.0	0.0	0.0	.2	0.0	0.0	0.0	.4	0.0

that are incomprehensible at these upper ages. Inspection of the data shows that the few children who continue to use incomprehensible responses at the upper age levels have a much higher mean number of syllables combined per response than do those of the younger ages.

CHRONOLOGICAL AGE AND SEX DIFFERENCES

The results of this construction analysis in relation to chronological age are shown in Tables XIX and XX and Figs. 12 and 13. Fig. 12 includes the incomprehensible responses, giving a total picture of the child's linguistic responses according to the construction analysis. Consideration of the comprehensible responses only (Table XX and Fig. 13) brings out the changes that occur with increase in chronological age much more clearly. It will be seen that the functionally complete but structurally incomplete responses constitute the major portion (75 per cent) of the comprehensible responses of the eighteen-months-old children. They decrease in relative amount with increase in age, but they continue as a large proportion of the responses in the upper ages, due to the increase in the number of answers. At twenty-four months the girls have fewer responses of this type than the boys, probably due to their more precocious development, and the dropping out of the single-word sentence as the word combinations begin to appear. They do not continue to have a smaller proportion of this category, however, in the upper age levels, because of the increase in the number of answers, which, as we noted in the previous chapter, were more numerous among the girls than among the boys.

The simple sentence without a phrase has already entered into the child's language by eighteen months but in very small proportions, for it constitutes only 6.7 per cent of the total number of responses of the boys and 4.2 per cent of the total number of responses of the girls of that age. These percent-

TABLE XIX

Mean Per Cent Each Item of the Construction Analysis by CA and Sex

CA	Sex	Funct. Compl.	Simple Sent.	Simple with Phrase	Comp. and Compl.	Elab. Sent.	Omis. of Verb	Omis. of Subj.	Misc. Omis.
18	B	10.7	.7	.0	.0	.0	.9	.0	1.8
	C	29.8	4.2	.0	.0	.0	2.2	.4	1.3
	All	21.2	2.6	.0	.0	.0	1.6	.2	1.4
24	B	33.3	5.3	.0	1.3	.0	2.5	.5	5.3
	G	37.2	15.6	1.5	.2	.7	8.8	1.3	12.2
	All	35.6	11.5	.9	.6	.4	6.3	1.0	9.4
30	B	28.9	42.1	4.8	.8	.0	9.9	1.3	5.5
	C	32.9	29.1	4.7	1.7	1.8	7.8	3.0	4.0
	All	31.3	34.3	4.7	1.3	1.1	8.7	2.3	5.1
36	B	27.5	35.1	6.2	1.3	1.5	8.0	2.9	6.0
	C	22.8	50.6	10.6	1.4	.9	5.1	3.6	4.3
	All	25.4	42.1	8.2	1.4	1.2	6.7	3.2	5.3
42	B	26.1	36.0	9.8	7.6	1.8	6.8	1.3	6.0
	C	35.3	31.8	13.0	4.5	2.8	5.0	2.5	5.0
	All	29.8	34.3	11.1	6.4	2.2	6.1	1.8	5.6
48	B	30.2	36.0	12.3	6.5	5.1	1.1	2.2	3.1
	C	31.0	42.1	9.7	5.8	4.0	2.7	3.1	1.3
	All	32.0	39.4	10.9	6.1	4.5	2.0	2.7	2.1
54	B	31.2	37.9	8.8	8.2	4.4	3.5	1.3	4.2
	C	31.1	34.7	12.2	5.6	7.8	2.4	3.1	3.1
	All	31.2	36.5	10.4	7.0	5.9	3.0	2.1	3.7

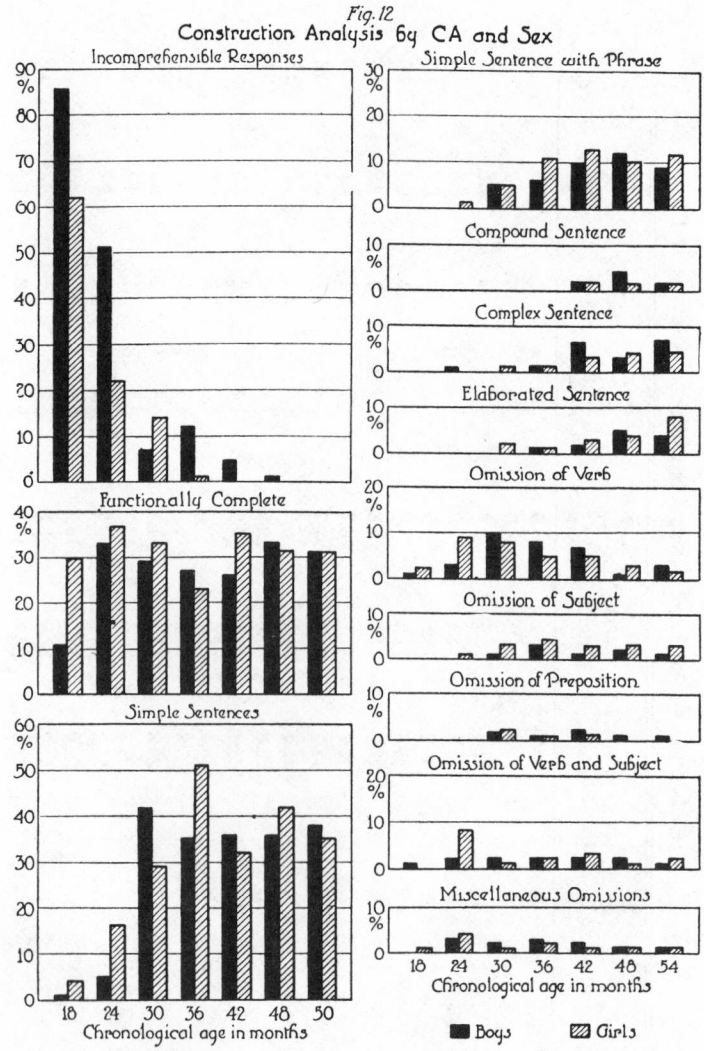

Fig. 12
Construction Analysis by CA and Sex

TABLE XX

MEAN PER CENT EACH ITEM OF THE CONSTRUCTION ANALYSIS BY CA AND SEX
(BASED ON COMPREHENSIBLE RESPONSES ONLY)

CA	SEX	FUNCT. COMPL.	SIMPLE SENT.	SIMPLE WITH PHRASE	COMP. AND COMPL.	ELAB. SENT.	OMIS. OF VERB	OMIS. OF SUBJ.	MISC. OMIS.
18	B	76.2	4.8	.0	.0	.0	6.4	.0	12.6
	G	78.5	11.0	.0	.0	.0	5.7	1.0	3.3
	All	78.4	9.6	.0	.0	.0	5.9	.8	5.2
24	B	67.9	10.7	.0	2.6	.0	5.1	1.0	10.7
	G	47.7	20.0	1.9	.2	.9	11.2	1.7	15.6
	All	53.8	17.3	1.4	.9	.6	9.4	1.5	14.2
30	B	31.1	45.3	5.1	.8	.0	10.6	1.3	5.9
	G	38.3	33.8	5.4	1.9	2.1	9.1	3.5	4.7
	All	35.3	38.7	5.3	1.5	1.2	9.8	2.6	5.7
36	B	31.2	39.9	7.0	1.4	1.7	9.1	3.3	6.8
	G	22.8	50.6	10.6	1.4	.9	5.1	3.6	4.3
	All	27.2	45.1	8.7	1.5	1.3	7.2	3.4	5.6
42	B	27.2	37.7	10.2	7.9	1.9	7.2	1.4	6.3
	G	35.3	31.8	13.0	4.5	2.8	5.0	2.5	5.0
	All	30.6	35.3	11.4	6.5	2.3	6.3	1.9	5.7
48	B	33.2	36.0	12.3	6.5	5.1	1.1	2.2	3.1
	G	31.0	42.1	9.7	5.8	4.0	2.7	3.1	1.3
	All	32.0	39.4	10.9	6.1	4.5	2.0	2.7	2.1
54	B	31.3	37.9	8.8	8.2	4.4	3.5	1.3	4.2
	G	31.1	34.7	12.2	5.6	7.8	2.4	3.1	3.1
	All	31.2	36.5	10.4	7.0	5.9	3.0	2.1	3.7

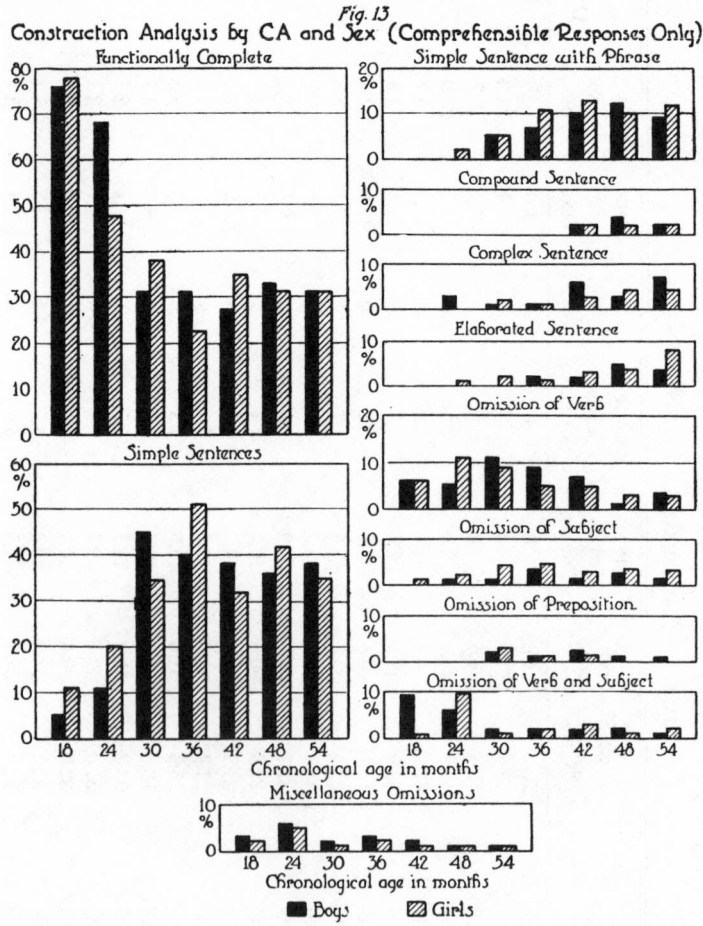

Fig. 13
Construction Analysis by CA and Sex (Comprehensible Responses Only)

ages become 4.8 per cent and 11 per cent, respectively, when we consider the comprehensible responses only. The girls are superior to the boys in the number of simple sentences at the younger ages, but in the upper age levels, when the girls are acquiring the more complex forms, the two sexes are about equal in the proportion of their conversation which consists of simple sentences.

The phrase was considered an added complexity in sentence formation, which it was thought it would be interesting to analyze separately. The next category in this classification, therefore, was the simple sentence with a phrase. The phrase first appears among the girls twenty-four months old (Fig. 12). They maintain a fairly consistent superiority over the boys in the proportion of simple sentences with phrases, until at fifty-four months 8.8 per cent of the total number of responses obtained from the boys and 12.2 per cent of those obtained from the girls belong in this category.

In accordance with the findings of Nice,[50] the compound and the complex sentences, which were the next two categories of this classification, were a very small proportion of the children's conversation at all age levels. Nice [50] says that only about one or two compound or complex sentences are found in fifty. · In the present investigation, compound sentences did not appear until the age of thirty months. They never exceed 4 per cent of the total number of responses at any age level, and no sex differences appear for this group. Complex sentences appear as a very small proportion at the age of twenty-four months. Their number remains small throughout, and no sex difference is noticeable.

The number of complex sentences given above is probably too small, since the sixth type of complete sentence—the elaborated sentence, which has been studied separately—includes the more involved of the complex sentences. As defined in Chapter II, the group of elaborated sentences includes those with two phrases, two subordinate clauses, or a phrase and a clause. Since many sentences that are technically complex, i.e., have one subordinate clause, may be quite short and are not characteristic of the most advanced type of sentence that children of these ages use, it was thought advisable to distinguish this more intricate type of response and to treat it in a separate analysis. Thus, the elaborated sentence group includes many complex sentences. The elaborated sentence first appears among the girls at twenty-four months, and among the boys it does not appear until thirty-six months. The group increases quite markedly with increase in age, the girls appearing slightly superior to the boys in the percentage of elaborated sentences. By fifty-four months, this group constitutes 4.3 per cent of the ·total number of responses of the boys and 7.8 per cent of the responses of the girls.

The remainder of the responses, that is, those that were not included in any of the above categories, were scored as incomplete sentences and classified according to the different types of omissions. It may be seen from inspection of Table XIX and Fig. 12 that incomplete sentences are a very small percentage of the total number of responses obtained from the eighteen-months-old children. This is because the responses that they gave were either incomprehensible or were single-word sentences, which were placed in the functionally complete but structurally incomplete category. In many cases their responses were not complicated enough to permit detection of omissions. The incomplete responses increase in relation to the percentage of complete responses through the twenty-four- and thirty-months- age levels when the children are using sentences that are sufficiently complete to allow detection of omissions. In the upper ages we note a decrease in the percentage of incomplete sentences, a true decrease, since by that time practically all the responses are comprehensible and sufficiently complete to permit detection of errors. Table XX and Fig. 13 bring out the trends with chronological age in a different light. They show the percentage of the comprehensible responses that are incomplete. When considered in relation to the comprehensible responses only, the tendency for the incomplete sentences to decrease with advance in chronological age is apparent.

Omission of the verb, that is, some essential part of the verbal combination, proved to be the most frequent type of omission at nearly all ages, but particularly in the lower age groups it constituted the major portion of the incomplete sentences. Omission of the subject comes next in importance, but it is relatively less important at the lower age levels in which the child is in the naming stage, and nouns, as will be brought out in the next chapter, are the most important part of speech in the child's vocabulary. After the verbs and other parts of speech come into the vocabulary in larger numbers, the omission of the subject is a more frequent type of grammatical error. The only other type of omission that is at all large is the omission of both the verb and the subject. None of the other types of omission occurred with sufficient frequency to indicate any trends with chronological age or sex.

PATERNAL OCCUPATION

We have already noted the more advanced linguistic development of the children of the upper occupational groups as compared with those of the lower occupational groups in the other two types of analysis used in this investigation. The third type of analysis has also been considered in relation to paternal occupation, in an attempt to determine whether or not the children of the upper socio-economic classes are also superior in the complexity of their sentence structure. In Table XXI and Fig. 14 we again note the difference, in favor of the upper occupational groups at all ages, in the percentage of comprehensible responses. Also, it is clear that the functionally complete but structurally incomplete responses are a larger proportion of the comprehensible responses of the children of the lower occupational groups at the younger age levels. In the higher ages this type of response is approximately 20 per cent greater among the children of the lower occupational groups, indicating a less mature stage of linguistic development among them.

TABLE XXI

MEAN PER CENT MAIN ITEMS CONSTRUCTION ANALYSIS
BY CA AND PATERNAL OCCUPATION

CA	OCCUP. GROUP	FUNC. COMPL.	SIMPLE SENT.	SIMPLE WITH PHRASE	COMP. AND COMPL.	ELAB. SENT.	IN-COM-PLETE
18	I, II, III,	25.0	4.0	0.0	0.0	0.0	4.4
	IV, V, VI,	17.4	1.2	0.0	0.0	0.0	2.0
24 and 30	I, II, III,	33.4	29.8	4.3	1.8	1.6	18.2
	IV, V, VI,	34.0	17.2	1.5	.3	.1	14.7
36 and 42	I, II, III,	20.4	44.5	13.2	6.3	2.9	12.4
	IV, V, VI,	34.7	32.4	6.3	1.6	.6	16.0
48 and 54	I, II, III,	20.5	41.7	12.3	12.3	6.3	6.7
	IV, V, VI,	37.4	34.5	9.1	5.6	4.2	8.8

The simple sentence constitutes a larger proportion of the conversation of the children of the upper occupational groups at the younger ages, when it is the most advanced type of response represented. However, at the higher ages, when more complex forms of sentences are appearing, the children of the upper occupational groups no longer maintain their superiority in this type of response.

The simple sentence with a phrase shows a consistent difference in favor of the upper occupational groups at all age levels. Likewise, the compound and the complex sentences are a much greater proportion of the conversation of the children from the upper groups than they are of the conversation of the children in the lower occupational groups. We also notice that the elaborated sentence shows similar differences

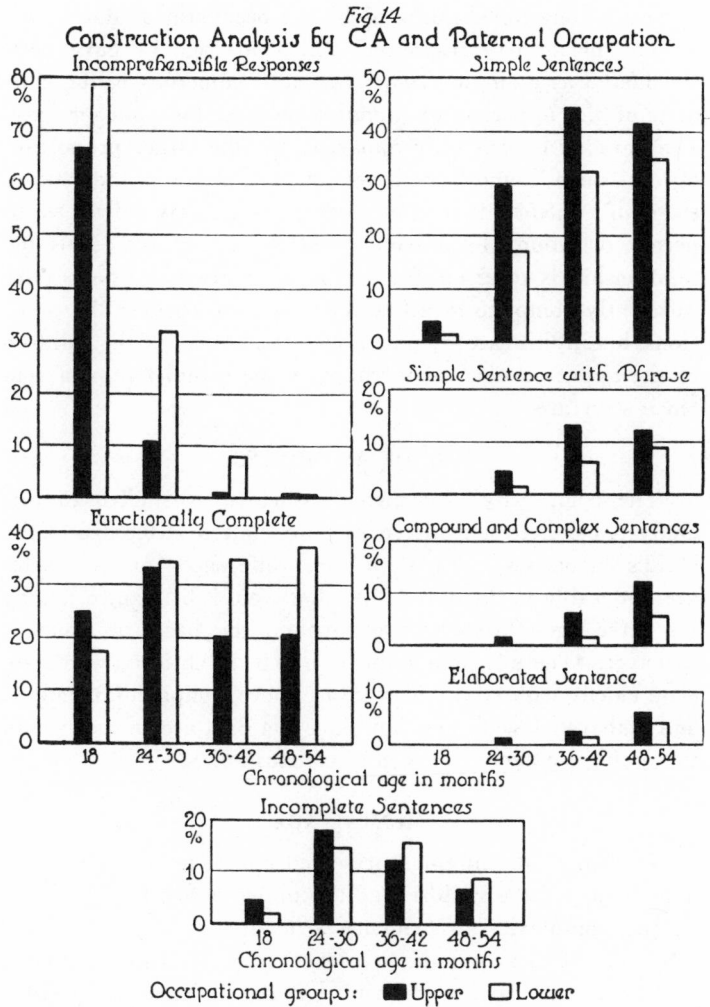

Fig.14

Construction Analysis by CA and Paternal Occupation.

Chronological age in months

Occupational groups: ■ Upper □ Lower

at all age levels, indicating a more precocious linguistic development among the children of higher occupational status.

The incomplete responses, which in Fig. 14 have been considered as a single group, are more numerous in the children of the upper occupational groups at the younger ages. The paradox here is only apparent, for the larger proportion of omissions found for these younger children indicates a stage of sentence formation that is sufficiently advanced to permit detection of omissions. At the upper age levels the relationship is reversed, for by that time all the responses are sufficiently complete to allow the scorer to discover the omissions, but in this case we note a true superiority of the children of the upper occupational groups in the completeness of sentence structure.

AGE OF ASSOCIATES

The complexity of sentence structure as studied in this analysis has been considered also in relation to the age of the child's associates. No significant differences or tendencies are noticeable in this tabulation that would distinguish among the three age-of-associates groups on the basis of sentence structure. There is some indication that the children who associate chiefly with adults tend to use more compound, complex, and elaborated sentences, but since the data are so meager on this point, we cannot draw any conclusions.

MENTAL AGE

In view of the findings presented above, indicating a clear superiority of the children of the upper occupational groups in the complexity of sentence structure, it was considered advisable to carry out the construction analysis in relation to mental age in order to determine if the differences that were found in relation to chronological age were due to the differences in the intellectual status of the two groups that we

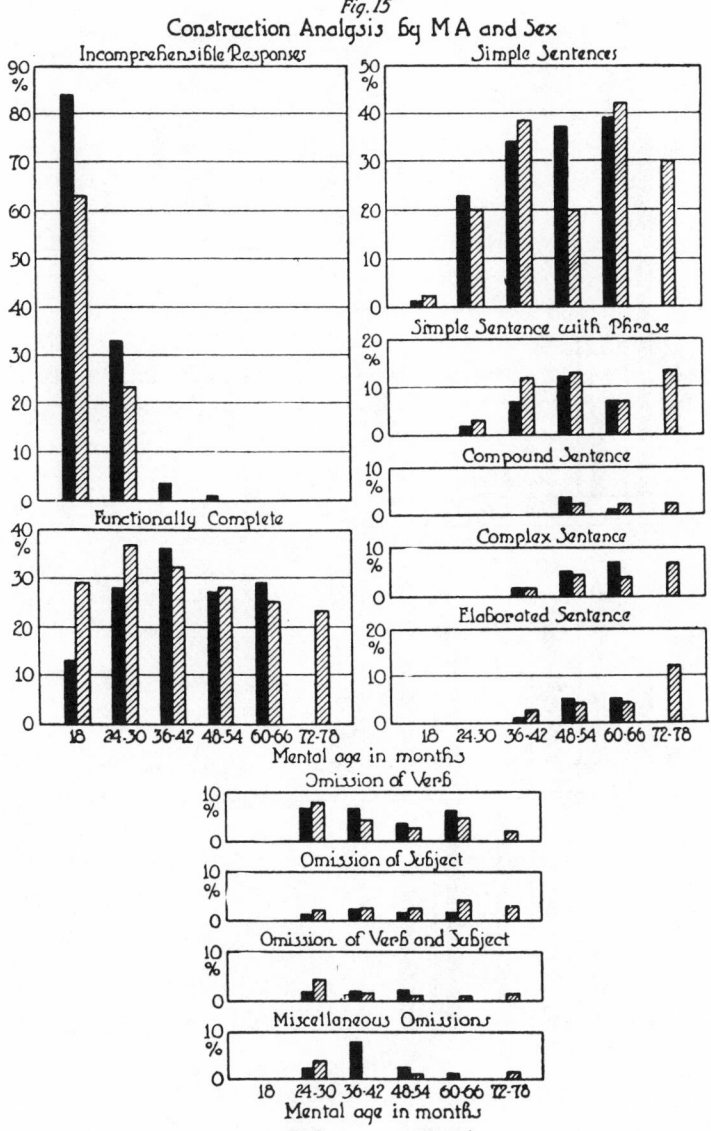

Fig. 15
Construction Analysis by M A and Sex

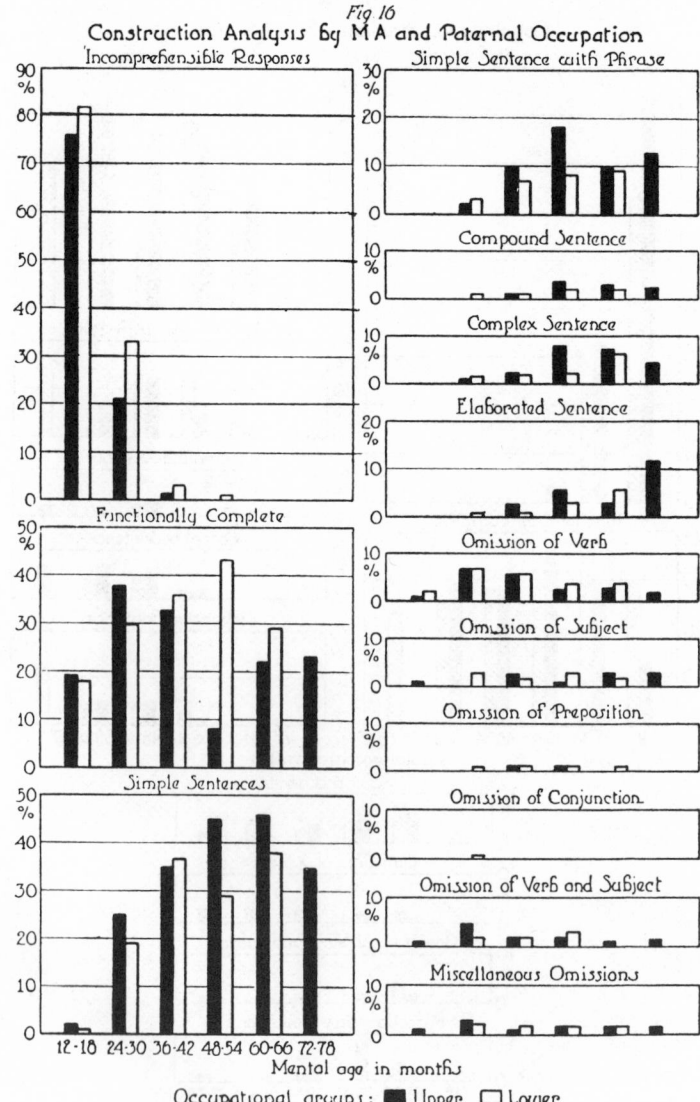

Fig 16
Construction Analysis by M A and Paternal Occupation

Occupational groups: ■ Upper □ Lower

have been comparing. Consideration of the mean per cent of each construction item according to mental age groups (Fig. 15) revealed the same sort of differences from one mental age level to the next, as were found with increase in chronological age. The sex differences, though not quite as marked, are still evident in this part of the analysis.

When considered in relation to mental age and to paternal occupation, as in Fig. 16, the construction items still show striking differences between the upper and the lower occupational groups, indicating a more precocious linguistic development among the members of the upper occupational groups.

The construction analysis was also carried out in relation to mental age and to the age of associates. No clear-cut differences among the age-of-associates groups appear in this analysis. However, this tabulation necessitated fine groupings, and the number of cases involved in many of the classifications was so small that no reliable tendencies could be expected to be revealed by this study.

SUMMARY

Classification of the children's responses according to their grammatical structure revealed the following tendencies:

1. A decrease in the relative number of the functionally complete but structurally incomplete responses with advance in chronological age.

2. An initial increase in the number of simple sentences.

3. An increase in the use of simple sentences with phrases with increase in age.

4. Increases in the percentages of compound, complex, and elaborated sentences with increase in age.

5. The incomplete responses at first are relatively small in proportion, then show an increase followed by a decrease in relation to the number of complete responses.

6. The girls show a clear superiority over the boys in all the items of this classification that show developmental tendencies.

7. The children of the upper occupational groups are markedly superior to those of the lower occupational groups in all of the items of the construction analysis.

8. The same tendencies appear in the construction analysis when it is considered in relation to mental age as were found in relation to chronological age, although the sex differences are less apparent.

9. No differences were brought out among the three age-of-associates groups on the basis of the complexity of grammatical structure.

10. The differences between the upper and lower occupational groups are still marked when mental age is constant.

CHAPTER VI

WORD ANALYSIS: PARTS OF SPEECH

As indicated in the introductory chapter, previous work on the language development of the child has been almost entirely concerned with the extent of vocabulary and with the proportions of the various parts of speech. Such studies, moreover, have dealt with only one or two children, a different method of counting words has been used in each study, and the children used were in all probability very precocious. No vocabulary studies have been carried out involving large numbers of children, much less, representative groups, so that no normative material is available. The previous investigations have attempted to record all the words that the child used, or, in some cases, all the words that the child understood and of which he knew the meaning. Since the criterion for including a word varied so greatly from one investigation to another—understanding of a word being sufficient for some, while others required not only use of the word by the child but its use "with meaning"; and since the lengths of the observation periods have varied—some taking down whole samplings of conversation, while others recorded merely the different words—from one hour to the all-day-conversation method, and even to the recording of the vocabulary over periods as long as three or four months, it is quite impossible to manipulate the material in the literature in any way that will give an adequate comparison between cases. Many of these records are very complete for the few children considered, but they tell us nothing about the vocabulary of the normal child of a certain age or about the progress in vocabulary from one age to another.

111

In the present study, while no attempt has been made to secure a complete record of each child's vocabulary, a sampling of each child's language has been obtained under the standardized conditions described above. A word analysis of these responses should give a picture of the total composition of the active vocabulary of each age level as it is obtained in a sample of running conversation. Characteristic samples of conversation from a number of children of the same age, and of children representing different age levels, should mean more than a complete record of the vocabulary of a single child, when we consider it in the light of normative material. According to the method used in this investigation, however, the particular words used were determined largely by the situation. For example, the nouns found in the lists of words are determined almost entirely by the toys presented in the experimental situation and by the objects in the pictures used. The results of this analysis, therefore, do not give any indication of the extent of vocabulary, but rather give a picture of the proportions of the different parts of speech, as they enter into representative samples of the child's running conversation, or his vocabulary as it is used, at the various age levels.

Throughout the tabulation of the words, the functional use of the word was regarded as the significant aspect to consider in the classification. All responses were therefore placed in the various categories of the different parts of speech, according to how they were used in the sentence. If the same word occurred as more than one part of speech, it was counted twice. Proper nouns were not counted as different words. Articles and numbers were included as adjectives. Childish forms of the same words were counted as different words; for example, "cat," "kitty," and "meow" (used as nouns) were scored as different words. A category of miscellaneous words was made necessary by the occurrence of a very small proportion of expressions which, as they were used by the children, did not seem to fit into any of the regular parts-of-speech categories, for example, "yes," "no," "kinda," "sure," and such expressions were placed in this group. All parts of verbal combinations were counted as separate words and as verbs; for example, "had been playing" counted as three separate words. Auxiliaries and participles always counted as verbs except when the latter were used as adjectives. The variants of verbs, adjectives, and pronouns were not counted as separate words unless they were irregular and the roots of the words were changed.

TABLE XXII

MEAN NUMBER OF WORDS AND MEAN NUMBER OF
DIFFERENT WORDS USED
BY CA AND SEX

CA	MEAN NUMBER OF WORDS			MEAN NUMBER OF DIFFERENT WORDS		
	Boys	Girls	All	Boys	Girls	All
18	8.7	28.9	20.3	5.4	13.6	10.0
24	36.8	87.1	66.0	16.6	37.3	29.1
30	149.8	139.6	143.7	52.8	49.8	51.0
36	164.4	176.2	170.3	60.1	66.0	62.8
42	200.8	208.0	203.7	76.7	90.6	82.3
48	213.4	218.5	216.3	91.1	93.8	92.6
54	225.4	236.5	230.5	95.8	104.0	99.5

TOTAL NUMBER OF WORDS USED

CHRONOLOGICAL AGE

The total number of words used by each child during the observations increases markedly with age, starting with 20.3 words at eighteen months and increasing to 230.5 words at fifty-four months, as is shown in Table XXII.

The percentages of the various parts of speech as found by this method were calculated on the total number of words

TABLE XXIII

Mean Per Cent of Each Part of Speech by CA and Sex
(Based on Total Number of Words Used)

CA	Sex	Nouns	Verbs	Adjec.	Adv.	Pronouns	Conjunct.	Prep.	Interj.	Misc.
18	B	43.6	16.7	5.1	5.1	12.8	.0	.0	16.7	.0
	G	51.5	13.1	10.7	8.5	9.8	.6	.0	5.5	.3
	All	50.0	13.9	9.6	7.9	10.3	.5	.0	7.6	.3
24	B	49.3	15.3	5.8	3.7	15.0	.0	2.0	3.4	5.4
	G	35.5	22.6	11.6	8.0	14.5	.7	4.1	2.2	.8
	All	38.6	21.0	10.3	7.1	14.6	.5	3.6	2.4	1.8
30	B	25.4	24.9	14.4	6.3	21.0	.5	4.3	1.5	1.8
	G	26.0	22.3	14.3	6.9	17.6	2.5	4.9	3.8	1.7
	All	25.8	23.4	14.3	6.7	19.0	1.7	4.6	2.8	1.8
36	B	23.6	23.5	15.4	7.8	21.3	1.1	5.4	1.5	.6
	G	23.2	22.5	16.7	6.3	17.3	3.7	8.4	1.5	.5
	All	23.4	23.0	16.1	7.0	19.2	2.4	6.9	1.5	.5
42	B	18.5	25.3	15.1	8.4	19.7	3.0	6.7	2.4	1.0
	G	18.5	27.0	16.6	7.0	21.8	1.3	5.8	1.6	.5
	All	18.5	26.0	15.7	7.8	20.3	2.3	6.3	2.0	.8
48	B	19.7	26.8	13.7	6.7	20.5	3.3	7.3	.9	1.0
	G	20.4	25.3	15.4	5.2	22.5	3.8	6.2	.6	.6
	All	20.1	26.0	14.6	5.9	21.6	3.6	6.7	.8	.8
54	B	19.4	25.0	14.4	7.7	21.1	4.0	6.7	.9	.8
	G	19.3	25.3	16.1	6.3	19.9	3.5	7.6	1.4	.6
	All	19.3	25.1	15.2	7.0	20.5	3.8	7.1	1.2	.8

used. It will be noted from Table XXIII and Fig. 17 that the
percentage of nouns, which is 50 per cent of the total number
of words used by the eighteen-months-old children, decreases
in relative amounts to about 19 per cent. The verbs, on the
other hand, increase from about 14 per cent to 25 per cent in

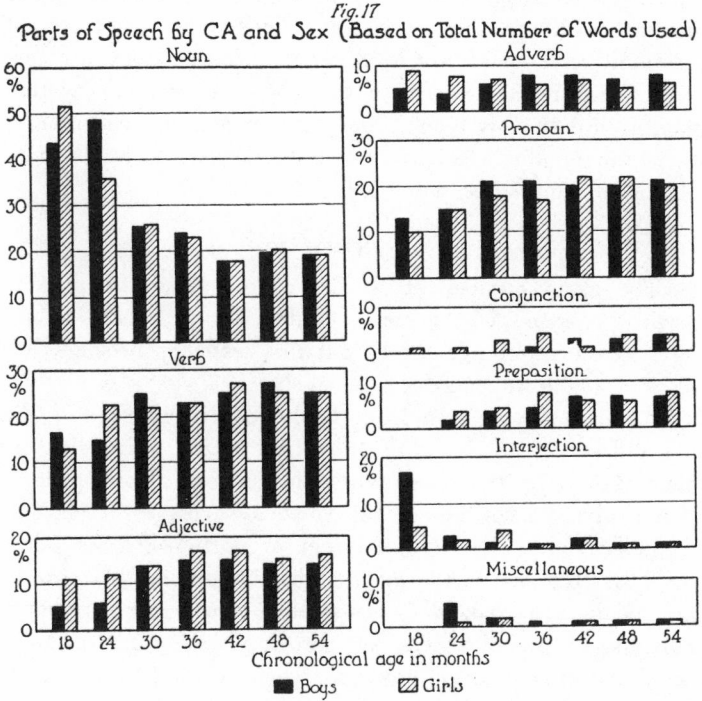

Fig. 17

Parts of Speech by CA and Sex (Based on Total Number of Words Used)

Chronological age in months

■ Boys   ▨ Girls

the age range. Adjectives almost double in the proportions
of the total number of words that they make up, as we go from
eighteen to fifty-four months. Adverbs show no consistent
tendency with increase in age, and they never exceed 9 per cent
of the total number of words used. Pronouns represent about
10 per cent of the total number of words used by the eighteen-

months-old children, and they increase to approximately 20 per cent of the words used by the fifty-four-months-old children. Prepositions do not appear at all among the eighteen-months-old children, and increase with age from about 3 per cent at two years to about 7 per cent among the older children. Conjunctions appear late, and although they show a steady increase with age, they never equal more than 4 per cent of the total number of words obtained. Interjections decrease with age from 16 per cent of the words of the boys eighteen months old to less than 1 per cent among the children of fifty-four months. The group of miscellaneous words is small at all ages and shows no trend with age.

SEX DIFFERENCES

The mean number of words secured from the girls is greatly in excess of the mean number of words used by the boys at the lower age levels, but this tendency becomes less marked at the upper ages.

As may also be seen from Table XXIII and Fig. 17, the sex differences in favor of the girls, which were noted in connection with the other types of analysis, also appear in this analysis according to the various parts of speech. At eighteen months they have a larger proportion of nouns than the boys, but this is the age at which nouns, as first words, are being acquired, and hence this relationship probably indicates a more advanced stage for the girls than for the boys. By the next age level, however, when the boys reach their maximum proportion of nouns, the girls have begun to show the decrease in the proportion of nouns that is the character-istic trend with increase in age. At the younger age levels, the girls excel the boys in the percentage of adjectives, but the two sexes are about equal in this respect by the age of thirty months. The same relationship between them may be noted for the adverbs as for the adjectives. No consistent difference appears in the proportion of the total number of pronouns used. Conjunctions appear as a very small proportion among the girls of the two youngest age levels, whereas they are not used at all by the boys until the age of thirty months. The girls are superior in the proportion of conjunctions used at the next two age levels, when they are just appearing in the vocabularies of the boys. After forty-two months, however, the two sexes are about equal in the number of conjunctions used in conversation. Prepositions, as mentioned before, do not appear among the children of eighteen months. No consistent sex difference appears in this part of speech, as there are several reversals of the direction of the difference from one age level to the next. Interjections are a much greater proportion of the active vocabularies of the youngest boys than they are of the vocabularies of the youngest girls, but this difference disappears as the children grow older. No sex difference appears in the small percentage of miscellaneous expressions used.

TOTAL NUMBER OF DIFFERENT WORDS USED
Chronological Age

It may also be seen from Table XXII that the mean number of different words used at each age level, in the specimens of conversation secured in this investigation, increases markedly with age throughout the age range that has been considered in this experiment. The percentage of nouns (Table XXIV and Fig. 18) used at each age level decreases with age also in the analysis according to the variety of words used but not nearly as much as when the total number of words used is considered. The increase in the relative importance of verbs is about the same as in the table (Table XXIII) previously discussed. Adjectives and adverbs show no definite trends with age in the table involving the variety of words

TABLE XXIV

MEAN PER CENT OF EACH PART OF SPEECH BY CA AND SEX
(BASED ON NUMBER OF DIFFERENT WORDS USED)

CA	SEX	NOUNS	VERBS	ADJEC.	ADV.	PRONOUNS	CONJ.	PREP.	INTERJ.	MISC.
18	B	37.2	11.6	18.6	4.7	14.0	.0	.0	4.7	9.3
	G	42.5	17.5	8.8	10.0	12.5	1.3	.0	3.8	3.8
	All	44.2	16.8	7.4	9.5	11.6	1.1	.0	4.2	5.3
24	B	42.4	22.8	5.4	5.4	14.1	.0	4.3	2.2	3.3
	C	38.2	28.6	11.6	4.5	9.0	1.0	3.5	2.1	1.5
	All	39.3	29.1	10.7	3.9	9.0	.9	3.4	2.6	1.3
30	B	35.2	24.6	12.1	6.5	9.6	1.5	5.5	2.0	3.0
	C	38.6	23.5	13.8	7.0	7.0	2.0	3.7	1.7	2.7
	All	40.4	24.3	12.0	6.6	6.0	1.6	4.3	1.6	3.0
36	B	40.7	22.9	13.5	7.4	8.1	1.0	4.0	1.3	1.0
	C	35.4	28.5	11.8	6.8	8.7	.8	4.6	1.5	1.9
	All	40.9	26.2	12.8	6.4	6.2	.7	4.0	1.7	1.2
42	B	40.1	27.4	10.6	7.4	5.5	1.6	4.0	1.6	1.9
	C	37.8	25.4	12.1	7.3	8.5	1.8	4.5	2.1	.6
	All	41.4	26.1	11.3	7.7	5.5	1.4	3.8	1.8	1.0
48	B	36.8	28.3	10.8	7.5	7.5	1.7	3.9	1.7	1.9
	C	38.0	28.0	11.1	7.7	6.7	1.5	3.9	.8	2.3
	All	39.8	28.4	11.9	7.3	5.6	1.1	3.3	.8	1.9
54	B	36.0	27.8	14.0	7.2	6.5	1.2	3.6	2.0	1.7
	C	36.8	25.5	12.5	8.5	7.1	2.4	3.8	1.4	2.1
	All	38.8	25.5	13.4	7.4	5.7	1.7	3.2	2.5	1.8

used. The pronouns in these considerations decrease in relative importance from about 15 per cent at the younger extremes to 7 per cent at the upper ages. While the conjunctions increase in absolute numbers with increase in chronological

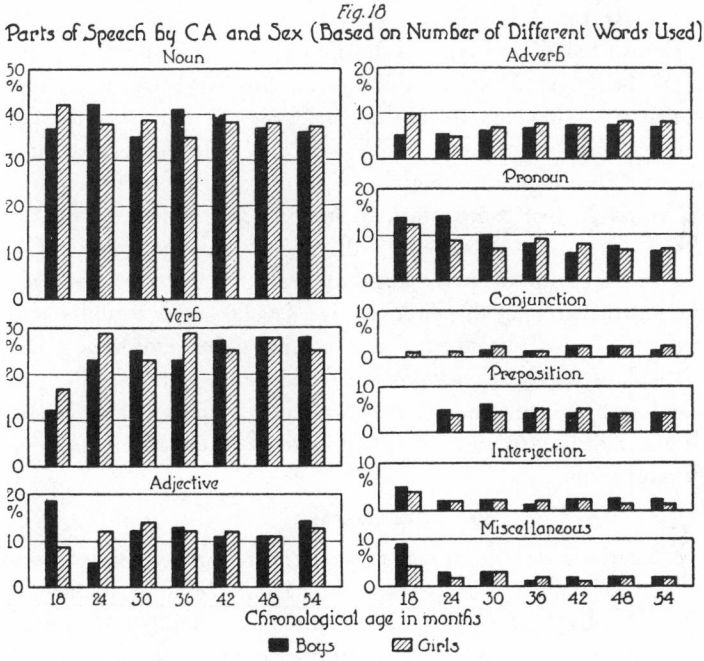

Fig. 18

Parts of Speech by CA and Sex (Based on Number of Different Words Used)

age, as do most of the other parts of speech, they show no increase when considered in relation to the other parts of speech, as represented by the percentage they are of the total number of different words used at each age level. Prepositions remain fairly constant in their relationship to the other parts of speech in these considerations. Interjections, however, decrease in proportion to the other parts of speech from eighteen to twenty-four months, and thereafter remain fairly constant.

SEX DIFFERENCES

Table XXII also shows that the difference between the sexes is more marked at the younger age levels when there is the most rapid rise in the whole vocabulary and when the girls are going through the developmental cycle more rapidly than the boys. The sex differences, however, are much less consistent from age to age in this type of analysis. In the younger age levels, the decrease in the percentage of nouns is more rapid among the girls. The increase in the percentage of verbs is also more marked among the younger girls, but these differences disappear with advance in age. Similarly, the increase in the percentage of verbs occurs more quickly among the girls at the younger age levels, but eventually this difference also disappears among the older children. The girls show a smaller proportion of pronouns than the boys at the lower age levels, and this tendency proved characteristic of the older children, and hence of a more advanced stage of development.

MENTAL AGE

Tabulations similar to those reported above have been made, considering the parts of speech in relation to mental age. In Table XXV are shown the mean number of words used at each mental age level and also the mean number of different words that occurred at each mental age level. It will be seen from this table that the average total number of words and the average number of different words used increase steadily with increase in mental age, even beyond the oldest chronological age group. While there are fairly consistent sex differences in favor of the girls, considering all the words used, these differences disappear in the table (Table XXIV) based on the different words used at an age level.

In Fig. 19, showing the parts of speech according to mental age, we see that at the mental age of exactly eighteen months as the mid-point of the interval, the proportion of nouns is slightly larger than that of the chronological age of eighteen months. It must be remembered in this connection that the children of the chronological age of eighteen months are slightly older than that mentally, as indicated by the IQ's presented in Chapter II. Hence we notice that the larger

TABLE XXV

MEAN NUMBER OF WORDS AND MEAN NUMBER OF DIFFERENT
WORDS USED BY MA AND SEX

MA	MEAN NUMBER WORDS USED AT EACH MA			MEAN NUMBER OF DIFFERENT WORDS USED AT EACH MA		
	Boys	Girls	All	Boys	Girls	All
12	0.0	0.0	0.0	0.0	0.0	0.0
18	9.6	29.3	38.9	3.0	8.7	5.2
24	46.5	60.3	106.7	15.3	11.6	8.9
30	112.9	124.6	237.5	21.6	18.4	14.5
36	169.8	207.7	377.5	28.6	45.2	24.3
42	173.4	181.4	354.9	37.1	35.0	26.1
48	228.7	198.4	427.1	48.2	42.9	32.9
54	239.2	266.8	506.0	46.7	49.0	33.8
60	234.0	235.3	469.3	50.2	71.7	43.1
66	231.0	244.8	475.8	87.0	67.0	77.6
72	....	246.5	246.5	....	84.5	84.5
78	....	292.5	292.5	....	90.0	90.0

percentage of nouns is characteristic of the children who are less mature mentally. Following through to the upper mental age levels, the decrease in the proportion of nouns continues through the seventy-eight-months level. Correspondingly, the percentage of verbs is smaller at the eighteen-months mental age level, and their proportion continues to increase throughout the mental age range represented in this study. It will be noted that two children eighteen months old in chronological age were retarded mentally so that they fell within the twelve-months mental age group. These two children had not yet begun to talk, so their utterances could not appear in these

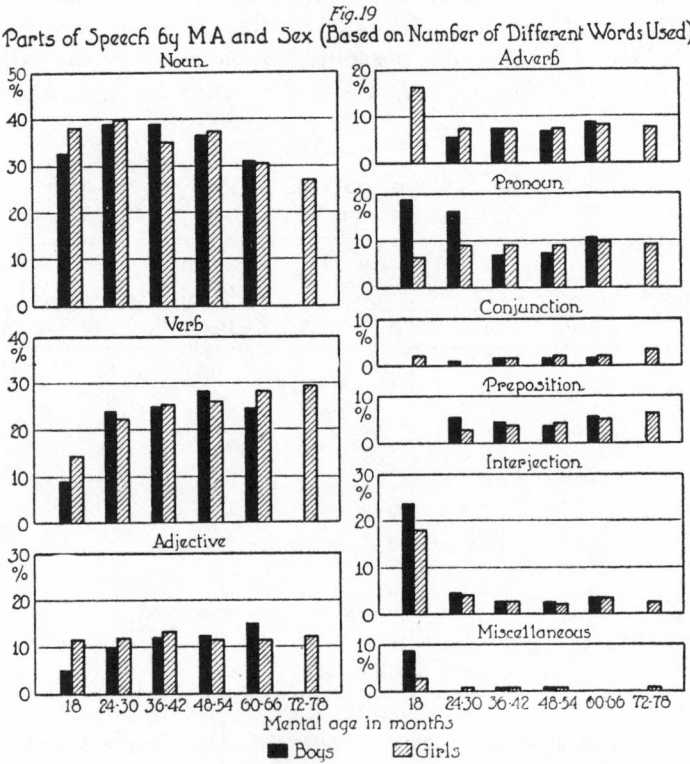

Fig.19
Parts of Speech by M A and Sex (Based on Number of Different Words Used)

analyses. Their vocalizations were entirely incomprehensible. Careful scrutiny of the other parts of this figure reveals the same trends which were noted in relation to chronological age, and which continue in the same directions at the upper mental ages. The sex differences in the proportions of the various

parts of speech are less apparent and probably non-existent
when mental age is held constant.

PARTS OF SPEECH BY PATERNAL OCCUPATION

In the light of Drever's [21] findings, mentioned in Chapter I,
it was thought that the data of the present problem might be
analyzed in order to contribute a little more information on
the factor of the influence of environment on vocabulary.
Therefore, the parts of speech were tabulated according to
paternal occupation as shown in Table XXVI. If Drever's [21]
point of view is correct, we should find in this analysis that
the children of the upper occupational groups, who supposedly
have broader environments, have a larger proportion of nouns
in their vocabularies. This does not prove to be the case in
the findings of the present investigation. The nouns are a
higher percentage of the total number of words used by the
children in this study who belong to the lower occupational
groups. This is in line with the other findings on occupational
group differences, for the smaller the percentage of nouns in
the vocabulary, the larger the percentage of the other types of
words, which show finer relationships and which indicate a
higher stage of linguistic development. Thus the children of
the lower occupational groups use vocabularies of the less
mature type than do the children of the upper occupational
groups. If we are justified in assuming that they have more
narrow environments than those of the upper social classes, it
seems that we have failed to confirm Drever's [21] theory, when
we measure the vocabularies by the total number of words
that occur in these samples.

The material presented in this chapter has many disadvan-
tages, several of which were brought out in connection with
the various vocabulary studies reported in the literature, for,
as the Whipples [75] say, the classification of children's vocabularies must always be somewhat artificial. In the first place,

TABLE XXVI

MEAN PER CENT OF EACH PART OF SPEECH BY CA AND PATERNAL OCCUPATION
(BASED ON TOTAL NUMBER OF WORDS USED)

PARTS OF SPEECH	CHRONOLOGICAL AGE							
	18		24 and 30		36 and 42		48 and 54	
	Occupational Group							
	Upper	Lower	Upper	Lower	Upper	Lower	Upper	Lower
Nouns	49.8	48.9	26.5	35.2	19.2	23.2	18.8	21.3
Verbs	17.1	7.2	23.5	21.0	24.7	23.7	25.9	24.7
Adjectives	8.2	12.4	13.1	12.1	15.6	16.7	14.1	16.1
Adverbs	8.6	6.5	6.6	7.6	7.2	8.3	7.2	5.5
Pronouns	10.0	10.9	20.0	14.2	20.9	18.0	22.2	19.0
Conjunctions	.4	.7	2.0	.4	3.0	1.5	3.3	4.3
Prepositions	0.0	0.0	4.7	4.0	7.4	5.8	6.8	7.1
Interjections	5.6	11.7	2.4	3.3	1.5	2.0	.9	1.1
Miscellaneous	.4	0.0	1.3	2.3	.6	.8	.7	.8

it was brought out that the first words of the child often function as whole sentences, or at least as more than one part of speech. Although we try to classify the words according to their function, it is often impossible to do so, especially when the word is used alone, and hence has to be classed as the part of speech under which it is first listed in the dictionary. As Lukens [38] points out, we probably are not justified in classing the child's words as parts of speech until he uses all the parts of speech correctly. The fact that this analysis has been carried down to the lower age levels, before all the parts of speech are represented, may account for the high proportion of nouns, and for the instability of the proportions of some parts of speech at the lower age levels and their relatively stable proportions at the upper ages.

The method used here does not attempt to give total vocabularies, but rather to measure language development by taking samples by the cross-section method. The fact that these children use such a variety of words in such a short observation period is in itself sufficient to disprove many of the extremely low estimates which have been made of children's vocabularies, and which have stimulated many of the vocabulary studies reported above. The figures have been presented here in both forms, i.e., according to the total number of words used and according to the number of different words used, in order to enable more comparisons to be made with other studies. The problem of whether or not to include variants is indeed questionable, as indicated by the Whipples,[75] but as has been pointed out, the method adopted for this analysis is that which has been most widely accepted in the literature, and upon which many of the published reports are based.

It is obvious that the proportions of the parts of speech according to the number of different words is determined largely by the proportions of the different parts of speech that are represented in the dictionary. In view of the findings of Kirkpatrick [36] we note that the proportions of the various parts of speech in the number of different words used, both in this study and in that of Zyve,[79] tend to correspond fairly closely to the proportions in the dictionary. When, however, we consider the active vocabulary, regardless of variety, that is, counting every word as often as it occurs, we get a much better measure of linguistic development in the sense that we have then counted a noun every time a noun is used, a verb every time a verb is used, etc., regardless of duplications; and the true proportions are recorded as they appear in the child's vocabulary, not as they are arbitrarily determined by the dictionary. This is seen by the fact that the changes with age appear so much more clearly in the analysis according to all the words used. There is a fairly close correspondence between the figures of the present study, using the percentages of the total number of words and those of Zyve's [79] study, in which third grade children were the subjects. This probably indicates that the children of the present investigation were selected so that the oldest subjects were at about the highest point of the curve in this developmental process of learning to talk, and that had we included older children, there probably would have been little increase in linguistic development beyond that shown by the oldest subjects of this experiment.

It has been shown in the foregoing paragraphs that in considering the parts of speech as they appear in the child's vocabulary, we are dealing with material that is rather questionable from the psychological standpoint. The question of the part of speech under which the single-word sentence is to be classed, the problem of the inclusion of variants of words, the use of the total number of words, or simply of the number of different words used—all make material of this sort rather elusive. It is well to note, however, in connection with the method used here, that essentially the same results have been obtained for this larger number of children, using only samplings of their speech recorded in a comparatively short period of time, as have been found for small numbers of children for whom very careful and detailed records were kept over long periods.   It would seem from such indications as these that nearly as good a measure of the child's linguistic status can be obtained by a series of short observations as by long-continued study.   This merely serves to show the value of the cross-section method in dealing with material of this sort; and is somewhat in line with the results of other studies being conducted at the Institute of Child Welfare at the University of Minnesota, in which a very high reliability has been found for daily one-minute observations of children in the nursery school, carried on for several months (the time required for the establishment of reliability varying with the function being studied).   If we can establish reliable methods for the short observations that are almost essential in dealing with the small child, the future holds much in store in the way of research and it is likely that by taking series of cross-sections of the same children at frequent intervals, we can approximate a longitudinal section of the developmental process.

CHAPTER VII

DISCUSSION

THEORIES OF THE ORIGIN OF LANGUAGE

Philosophers and philologists have long debated the problem of the origin of language. The result seems to be a confusion of isolated theories, with varying degrees of plausibility and adequacy, but none with any definite proof. The future holds little promise for an adequate solution of this problem from a phylogenetic standpoint, for as has been aptly remarked, language has left no fossils. The comparative philologist has little concrete evidence in his science analogous to that found in the science of archeology. The only approach that may prove fruitful seems to be the study of the languages of primitive peoples, but even their languages have already originated and are far advanced before we begin to study them, and there too, we have to revert in large measure to the ontogenetic attack on the problem.

One of the simplest theories, and one which we find mentioned very often in the literature, is the onomatopœic theory, or as it is nicknamed, the "bow-wow" theory, which Noire [52] attributes to Herder. According to this theory, language originated by the designation of objects by the noises they made; for example, "bow-wow," "meow," "moo-moo," "coo-koo," and the like are considered to have been the first sort of words invented by primitive man, and also the first kind of words used by the child. In short, this theory holds that man adopted the cries of animals as signs. Noire [52] says, however, "This theory, however plausible and seductive it may seem at first sight, is directly opposed to the facts of any language yet examined." He thereupon quotes Max Müller, who says:

Our answer is . . . . that though there are names in every language formed by mere imitation of sound, yet these constitute a very small proportion of our dictionary. They are the *playthings*, not the *tools*, of language, and any attempt to reduce the most common and necessary words to imitative roots ends in complete failure.

On the other hand, we find that Robinson and Robinson [60] quote Jesperson, who discredits Max Müller's remarks, and who in speaking of the onomatopœic theory of language origin says:

Sounds which in one creature were produced without any meaning, but which were characteristic of that creature, could by man be used to designate the creature itself (or the movement or action productive of the sound). In this way, an originally unmeaning sound could in the mouth of an imitator and in the mind of someone hearing that imitation acquire a real meaning. I have tried to show how from the rudest and most direct imitations of this kind we may arrive through many gradations at some of the subtlest effects of human speech, and how imitation, in the widest sense we can give to this word—a wider sense than most advocates of the theory seem able to imagine—is so far from belonging exclusively to a primitive age that it is not extinct even yet.

After giving examples of the possibilities of word formation by this method, he says, "Echoic words may be just as fertile as any other part of the vocabulary."

Whether or not all language originates in this way is not for us to determine here, but in the vocabularies of little children there is found abundant evidence in favor of this theory. We have only to mention the frequent occurrence, among children, of such expressions as "tick-tock," "choo-choo," "bow-wow," "meow," "ding-a-ling," "moo-moo," and the like, and to consider the important place they occupy in the small vocabulary of the young child, to realize that this theory probably accounts for the origin of some, but not all, of language. It is difficult to determine, however, how often children use these expressions spontaneously as true examples of onomatopœia, and how much of this type of language is acquired in exactly the same way as more conventional types of words, that is, merely by hearing baby-talk spoken to them. As many of these terms have been accepted in what might be called the "dictionary of baby-talk," they are quite universally used by adults in speaking to children. The question then arises as to how these responses came to be universally accepted in the language, and here again we may have to return to the ingenious theory of their onomatopœic origin.

Another theory of the origin of language very frequently found in the literature is the interjectional theory, which Noire [52] says Max Müller has aptly called the "pooh-pooh" theory. As Chamberlain [12] mentions, "According to Zanardelli the language-unit is the interjection." This theory is based on the assumption that language is derived from the natural expressive cries and instinctive utterances. This hypothesis, however, has not withstood the onslaught of comparative philology, for as Leibnitz (Noire,[52]) has said, "If the constituent elements of human speech were either mere cries or the mimicking of the cries of nature, it would be difficult to understand why brutes should be without language," for they have indeed a great variety of natural cries that never develop into a system of language. Moreover, as has been pointed out by other writers, the interjection really is quite isolated from language proper, and does not enter into relation with other parts of speech. In the quotation from Jesperson referred to above [60] we also find reference to this interjectional theory.

The adherents of this theory generally take these interjections for granted, without asking about the way in which they have come into existence. Darwin, however, in *The Expression of the Emotions*, gives purely physiological reasons for some interjections. . . . . To the ordinary interjectional theory it may be objected that the usual interjections are abrupt expressions for sudden sensations and emotions; they are therefore isolated in relation to the speech material used in the rest of language. "Between interjection and word there is a chasm wide enough to allow us to say that the interjection is the negation of language, for interjections are employed only when one either cannot or will not speak." This "chasm" is also shown phonetically by the fact that the most spontaneous interjections often contain sounds which are not used in language proper . . . . whence the impossibility properly to represent them by means of our ordinary alphabet. . . . . On the other hand, many interjections are now more or less conventionalized, and are learnt like any other words, consequently with a different form in different languages: in pain a German and a Seelander will exclaim *au*, a Jutlander *aus*, a Frenchman *ahi* and an Englishman *oh*, or perhaps *ow*.

In spite of these criticisms, however, the large proportion of interjections found in the utterances of the young child, by practically all investigators shows how easily this theory originated. Nearly all students of child language report a very large proportion of interjections in the child's language, a proportion which decreases markedly with increase in chronological age. Moore [46] says of her son that his words were used like so many exclamations by which he announced the presence of something interesting. She also reports that interjections rank second among the various parts of speech in order of acquisition. Nice [51] reports that her child used 3.7 per cent interjections at eighteen months of age and only .9 per cent at the age of three years. These figures bring out the importance of interjections in the child's language, especially when we note the small number of them which are found in the language.

The percentage of interjections used by the child in his conversation mounts quite markedly when we consider the functional use of the words, for the younger children, who are just beginning to talk, frequently use nouns and other parts of speech, with interjectional inflections. Since function is the criterion of classification in the present study, the proportion of interjections is still higher than in other investigations. Considering the total number of words used, we find that children of eighteen months of age use approximately 8 per cent interjections, and considering the number of different words used, this figure mounts to approximately 10 per cent of their vocabularies at this age. (See Figs. 17 and 18.) Such findings might lead us to believe that there is some truth in the hypothesis; not that this theory in itself is adequate to explain the origin of all language, but that it may serve as an explanation of the acquisition of certain parts of language.

Many writers set forth another type of theory of the origin of language, which appears under a variety of names, but which amounts to the same thing in its essentials. Perhaps the term most widely used is the "pleasure-pain" theory. O'Shea [53] says that the motive for all the infant's vocal expression is to secure relief from discomfort. Hinckley [31] says that Schultze is supported by Gutzmann in his theory of the principle of least effort in the origin of language, but that he is opposed by Hall, Ament, and Rzesmtzek. The same type of idea is expressed by the Whipples [75] when they say, "It is doubtless true, as several writers have asserted, that ease of pronunciation is a determining factor in the acquisition of a vocabulary, but it is also true, as has been shown by Humphreys and the Gales that, after the second year, serviceability is a more important factor than ease of pronunciation." Bateman [5] also emphasizes the factors of serviceability and interest in accounting for the acquisition of the first words. Many writers have listed children's words according to their initial sound, and have thus tried to test this theory of ease of pronunciation. Certainly the easier words appear first, if we consider the length of the first words, but are we justified in saying that the first words are the easiest to pronounce? In the first place, we do not know what sounds are easiest for the child to pronounce. Our only criterion would be the order of their appearance, but this would assume the theory that we are seeking to test. If those who report the wide variety of sounds in the babbling stage (many of which drop out when true language appears) are right, then, from his wide and varied practice in the babbling stage, the child should be able to pronounce almost any sound easily at first, and the later development in this direction would be by more complex groupings of sounds into longer words.

Then, too, we find mentioned in the literature some more naïve types of explanation. One of these is the theory of invention—that primitive men set about deliberately to invent a language to meet their needs of communication. Somewhat in line with this is the theory of proper names, which Noire [52] attributes to Condillac and to Adam Smith, in which there was a tacit agreement between two savages to denote certain objects by certain sounds.

Noire's [52] theory, which has been nicknamed the "Yo-he-ho" theory, maintains that it is a relief to the system to let the breath be expelled strongly and repeatedly under strong muscular exertion. The sounds thus made become associated with the objects and events that occur simultaneously with them.

There are other theories of language, but they are all inadequate and most of them less plausible than those here mentioned. As has been pointed out, each theory explains only a part of language. They are for the most part individualistic and do not take into consideration the primary purpose of human language—that of social intercourse. Each theory explains only a very small proportion of language; that is, the interjections are accounted for, the few names of an onomatopœic origin have been accounted for, but the great bulk of language, and particularly the words that express the fine inter-relationships in sentence structure, is left out of the considerations entirely. It is indeed a far cry from the language that has as its sole origin the onomatopœic reproduction of primitive cries of animals, to the involved, abstract language of law or to the heights of classic poetry. Probably, we need to combine all the proposed theories, for each seems to have a grain of truth; but also we need to seek further for more adequate explanations, for as yet we have found explanations for only a very small part of the complex system of language.

THE RÔLE OF IMITATION

As indicated in Chapter I, many writers on the problem of the development of child language emphasize the importance of the factor of imitation in the process of learning to talk. O'Shea [53] says that the infant's first verbal imitations are concerned primarily with motor processes to make up words. Pollock [57] says, in speaking of children of seventeen or eighteen months, that the vocabulary is increasing fast, and almost any word proposed to the child is imitated with some real effort at correctness. Preyer [58] tells us that in the fourth quarter of the first year, we may perceive that sounds uttered are influenced by the sounds heard from other persons, and he speaks of this as the critical point in the learning of language. Stern [63] mentions that the essential factor of human speech development is the combined action of imitation and spontaneity. Thus, it is clear that it is generally recognized that something called imitation enters into, and plays a large part in, the learning of language by the child.

It is necessary, however, at the outset to distinguish what is meant by imitation and also to distinguish the two chief types of imitation that the child exhibits. There is, in the first place, the very narrow definition of imitation in which are included only exact reproductions of actions or sounds performed before the child. This exact, mimetic type of imitation is very rare but probably does occur in some instances. What is usually meant by imitation, however, is the attempt to reproduce the action seen, regardless of the accuracy or the success of the reproduction. This attempt at reproduction is very characteristic of young children, and it is a trait that has been noted by most observers of child life. It is probably most frequent in the field of vocal reproduction of sounds, or, if not, it is in this field that it is most easily noted.

The question now arises—what is the rôle of this factor of imitation in the learning of the complex system of habits that we call language? We know that it does enter into the process, since the child, regardless of the country of his nativity or of his parentage, learns the language that he hears spoken by those around him when he arrives at the age when he is able to note the sounds made by others and to attempt to imitate them himself. Moreover, in this connection, we have the evidence that the deaf child does not learn language because, on account of his handicap, he is unable to utilize this ability to imitate. All such evidence would lead us to believe that the child learns the actual words of language, in fact all the elements of language, by the use of this factor of imitation. However, it is interesting to note that Preyer [59] points out that, "mobility and perfection in the *technique* of sound-formation are not speech. They come into consideration in the process of learning to speak as facilitating the process because the muscles are perfected by previous practice." And further, he states, in this connection, "The formation of ideas is not bound up with the learning of words, but is a necessary prerequisite for the understanding of words to be learned first, and therefore for learning to speak." Taine [66] after describing the spontaneous "twittering" of his little girl, says, "She has learned only the materials of language." He then tells how, when two sounds that she had discovered by herself were repeated to her several times,

She listened attentively and then came to make them immediately she heard them. . . . . In short, example and education were only of use in calling her attention to the sounds that she had already found out for herself, in calling forth their repetition and perfection, in directing her performance to them, and in making them emerge and survive amid the crowd of similar sounds. But all initiative belongs to her.

This is essentially the conclusion that most psychologists are coming to at the present time in most of our modern textbooks. Here, however, we find it very clearly stated by Taine [66] as early as 1877. We are now rediscovering this conclusion that he deduced from his careful observations of his child and are couching it in modern terminology, which is hardly any clearer than the old mode of expression.

We now maintain that it is extremely doubtful whether the child learns any new elements by imitation. It is quite generally held that all the elements for the formation of language are present in the primitive babblings of the child, that the behavior of others merely serves to attract his attention· to the significant sounds in his repertoire, and that the repeated attempts to reproduce sounds made by others bring about the fixation of the response. It is obvious, however, that the child's first linguistic imitations are not all perfect mimetic reproductions, so that if we were to accept perfect reproduction as the only criterion of true imitation, we would have to say that this type of imitation does not necessarily, though it may, enter into the learning of language, and that most language acquisition occurs without this type of imitation. Admitting the broader interpretation of the term, it is clear that imitation in the sense of the attempt at reproduction does play a very important part in the learning of language. Tanner [67] points out that "after the child by his instinctive babblings and persistent imitation has learned to speak words, he learns to use them with a significance from constantly hearing one word used in connection with a given object." Until this association is formed, however, the child's imitative words are no more than the imitative words of the parrot.

Not only in the field of language has imitation been studied but in many purely motor functions as well. In all of these studies the conclusion emerges that the child is not able to acquire new behavior patterns by imitation if the elements for them are not already part of his reaction system. The child is unable to imitate actions that he has never before performed by himself. If, however, the elements involved in the performance have previously been used by him, he is able to combine these elements in new ways by the use of imitation. The behavior of others serves only to direct his attention to the significant elements and to show how they can be recombined effectively in new situations. Allport [1] says regarding this point:

If the ear-vocal reflexes have been sufficiently established for the sound of a word to call forth the response of articulating it, it is no longer necessary that the child himself should speak the stimulating word. It may be spoken by another. The effect will then be that of a child repeating the sounds which he hears others utter. . . . . The child does not imitate or duplicate the speech of his elders. There is evoked simply the nearest ear-vocal reflex which, with his present limitations of pronouncing, he has been able to fixate. The word "doll," spoken by the parent, would probably be repeated as *da* (*a* as in father). In this manner whole phrases far beyond the learner's comprehension may be reiterated rote fashion with as fair accuracy as the speech habits already acquired permit. It is essentially a parrot stage. In popular parlance it is known as "learning by imitation." The term "imitation" is, however, both inexact and misleading, for it suggests that the process is one of learning the speech of others by voluntarily copying them; whereas it is really the touching off of *previously acquired* speech habits by their conditioning auditory stimuli.

LANGUAGE AND THOUGHT

All through the history of philosophy we find that men have puzzled over the problem of the relationship between thought and language. In practically all instances it has been held that the relationship is a very close one. Just as the culture of a people is judged in large measure by the literature that it has produced, so the thought of an individual is usually considered to be revealed by his language. We have all noticed that when a person thinks very hard about something, he usually vocalizes about it; that is, he expresses his thoughts in language. Magni [40] quotes several writers who indicated an interest in this problem. Among them he says that Von Humboldt considers language the primitive organ of thought. He also quotes Kirkpatrick as saying that the vocabulary of a person represents in condensed form all that he has experienced and imagined. The breadth of his mental experience is indicated by the number of words that have meaning for him, while the accuracy of his thinking is shown by the exactness of meaning with which he uses words. Laurie is also quoted by the same author as expressing the view that by adding to the child's stock of understood words, we add to his stock of understood things and consequently to his material for thought. Taylor is also mentioned as indicating that the children's knowledge and their vocabularies grow at approximately the same rate, revealing the function of language in acquiring knowledge. Titchener [70] points out, "The spoken word is the medium of thought, as the visual idea is the medium of imagination. Hence the problem of the origin and development of language is one of prime importance for psychology." Wundt [76] also states that "the order of the words corresponds to the succession of ideas."

It is on the basis of such statements as these, and on the basis of the observation of some of the phenomena from which ideas are derived, that the identity of thought and language has been proposed by the behavioristic school, and it has since become one of the chief issues among the various schools of psychology. Watson [71] is the chief formulator of the theory and is the one against whom most of the attacks have been directed by its adversaries. Before this point of view was so

definitely set forth by Watson, there was considerable disagreement on the point among the writers on the subject. Dewey [18]
states that language is not thought but that it is necessary for
thinking as well as for its communication. Taine,[66] who, as
we noted in the preceding section, expressed such modern
ideas on the problem of imitation, also attacked this problem
of the relationship of thought and language as early as 1876.
Let us quote his concise statement:

Les concepts sont-ils possibles . . . . sans une forme extérieure et
un corps? Je réponds décidément *non*. . . . . Il n'y a pas de
pensée sans mots. . . . . Nous pouvons, par abstraction, distinguer
entre les mots et la pensée, mais nous ne pouvons jamais séparer l'un
de l'autre sans les détruire tous les deux. . . . . Nous ne trouvons
jamais dans la nature une pensée sans mots ou des mots sans pensée.

Here again, though Watson has caused a controversy over the
question, he has given us nothing new.

Watson [71] expresses the point of view that thinking is
merely the action of language mechanisms, that language
habits are merely substitutes for bodily response and are
short-cuts for the long ways of expression by explicit bodily
habits. Thinking consists of implicit language habits or
talking to ourselves. In some of his earlier work he gives the
impression that he maintains that all thinking is the action of
only the laryngeal mechanisms. However, in his book entitled
Behaviorism (1925), he says:

I wish here expressly to affirm that in developing this view I have
never believed that the *laryngeal movements* as such played the pre-
dominating rôle in thought. I admit that in my former presentations
I have, in order to gain pedagogical simplicity. expressed myself in ways
which can be so interpreted. We have all had the proofs before us time
and again that the larynx can be removed without completely destroying
a person's ability to think. Removal of the larynx does destroy articulate
speech, but it does not destroy whispered speech. . . . . My theory
does hold that the muscular habits learned in overt speech are respon-
sible for implicit speech (thought). It holds, too, that there are hun-
dreds of muscular combinations with which one can say either aloud or

to himself almost any word, so rich and so flexible is language organization and so varied are overt speech habits.

Watson admits that the evidence is largely theoretical but immediately points to the child who he says talks to himself constantly when alone. He also points to the adult who still talks to himself or who uses his lips in reading or thinking.

On the other hand, we find a great many statements to the contrary, for Preyer [59] states, "From this behavior of infants born deaf it manifestly follows that even without the possibility of natural imitation of sounds, and without the knowledge of a single word, qualities may be blended with qualities into concepts. *Thus, primitive thinking is not bound up with verbal language.*" He also informs us that "it was not language that generated the intellect; it is the intellect that formerly invented language."

In Helen Keller's autobiography there is evidence of thought without words, for after she was able to communicate her thoughts she gives descriptions of her thoughts before she knew any words. In one such statement she says, "I knew that I was going out into the warm sunshine. This thought, if a wordless sensation may be called a thought, made me hop and skip with pleasure." Again, she remarks after her discovery that everything had a name, "Each name gave birth to a new thought." She also states, "My thoughts would often rise and beat up like birds against the wind; and I persisted in using my lips and voice."

Watson [71] and some of his behavioristic followers would say in this connection that in the normal person we have thought going on as the action of language mechanisms, but in the deaf child other groups of muscles can take over the function and produce the short-cut behavior patterns. As Smith and Bartlett [65] point out in criticizing Watson's early position, "Many other bodily processes besides movements of the vocal musculature may take part in expressing language."

They state also that while all substitute signs may be treated as language, some only function as expressing thought, and hence some language habits are not thought—in short, that all language is not thought. Mere repetition of catchwords and phrases they say, does not represent thought; and again, that which is in origin thought, may by repetition become habitual, and the same word responses may or may not indicate thinking. They state further that perhaps, whenever we think, we employ language in some form or other, but that this does not prove that the act of thinking and the language movement are the same. Sully,[64] however, seems to agree with the modern point of view when he says that language is sound molded into definite forms and so made vehicular of ideas, and that to speak is to use sound intentionally as the sign of an idea. Carr [11] also expresses a similar attitude when he says that "language might well be defined as a device for thinking publicly, ... to express thoughts to others, and naturally there is no reason why the same device should not be employed in thinking privately."

Piaget [56] and many others attempt to study the child's thought and his logic through a study of his language. While this is probably the most satisfactory method with which we are now familiar, it has certain definite and serious limitations. In the first place we can hardly study the thought processes of the adult adequately by the method of verbal report. We can never be sure that another person has the same connotation for a word that we have. For him it may be a broader or a narrower term than it is for us, but in the case of the adult we can to some extent overcome these difficulties by using more language to define our terms. The introspectionists have found this a serious problem and hence have admitted only the work of trained observers, who, by a great deal of training involving similar experiences and practice, have come to have, as nearly as possible, the same connotations for the terms they use.

In the case of the child, however, this difficulty is much more serious, for the child, by reason of his extremely limited experience at the time that he begins to use language, has very different connotations for words than we have. Taine [66] reminds us that the child attaches to words ideas that we do not expect, and that he spontaneously generalizes. At times also the child invents a word, and we find, too, the obliteration of old words and their replacement by new ones. Also, he says that many meanings may be given to the same word by a child. The literature is full of anecdotes illustrating this point. The child who originally applies the word "daddy" to his father only, later uses the name for his uncles as well, and later still as the name for all men. When he learns the more specific terms as his vocabulary increases, the word "daddy" reverts to its original meaning, for he now knows the words "uncle" and "man" and can use them in the proper situations. In considering the objective facts of the child's language, there is no certainty as to how general or how specific his use of a term may be. This problem is still more difficult in the case of the child than in the case of the adult, for he is as yet unable to define his terms for us. Thus, while the child may think in words, we are on very uncertain ground when we try to study his thought processes through his language.

Watson [74] also, in addition to identifying thought and language, says that all memory occurs through our language mechanisms. He contends that there is no verbal memory before the third year, and that there is no memory of events before the child has begun to verbalize about his experiences. Many are inclined to doubt the theory that there is no thinking without words. They say that they often have thoughts which they are unable to express in words. This sort of phenomena would be explained by Watson in his *Unverbalized in Human Behavior* [74] as situations, objects, or events to which we had reacted only in a visceral or purely emotional way. There was merely an emotional tone to the situation, and no verbal or language habits were built up around it.

As previously mentioned, Watson [73] admits that most of the evidence for his point of view is theoretical. The only experimental evidence is a study by Wyczoikowska,[77] an unpublished study by Lashley, and also a conflicting piece of work by Thorson.[69] In Wyczoikowska's [77] experiment the subjects were asked to say the words, "experimental psychology," and also to think the same words while their tongue movements were graphically recorded. When the words were merely thought, the same sort of movements, but of smaller magnitude, occurred as when they were spoken. Lashley's study, as reported by Watson,[73] shows essentially the same results. Watson [73] thinks that this is evidence that the language mechanisms are used in thinking, even though these measurements of the minute tongue movements are very rough. Thorson's [69] work, which was done under Lashley, and which the latter considers a better controlled experiment than his, failed to confirm the previous findings. Watson,[72] however, says that while her (Thorson's,[69]) technique was adequate to give positive results, her failure to find them does not disprove the theory, since she was endeavoring to measure the tongue movements, which he says may be too gross. He would look for experimental confirmation of his theory in laryngeal movements and in movements of other parts of the language mechanism. Thus, the theory is still a question upon which further experimental work needs to be done before it can be accepted or rejected.

RESULTS OF THE PRESENT STUDY

The investigation described in the previous chapters has a purely factual basis, and no problems of such theoretical nature as those just discussed have been attacked in the present instance. This study has been rather an attempt to study the language of the little child as it is used by him in his everyday life. The method of direct observation has been used in an attempt to get a cross-section of the child's running conversation, from which we can study the length of response, the situations in which the child uses verbal responses, and the complexity of these responses in grammatical structure. Also, the material of this study lends itself very readily to word analyses and studies of the proportions of the various parts of speech which the child uses in his conversation.

Since this problem is essentially one of genetic psychology, and children of such varying ages have been used as subjects, the beginnings of speech and the complexities of sentence structure, as well as the new uses of language responses that appear with increased chronological age, are of particular interest here. Some of the facts that were brought out in preceding chapters with regard to some of the other variants considered, merit further discussion at this point.

SEX DIFFERENCES AND MENTAL AGE

Throughout the results of the investigation there were consistent sex differences in favor of the girls, not only in the length of response, but in the types of response in the functional analysis and in the construction analysis that were characteristic of the older children, and hence indicated a more advanced stage of linguistic development. Their superiority again appeared in the proportions of the various parts of speech in the word analysis. As presented in Chapter II, the girls had a higher mean IQ at nearly every age level. This is in accordance with the findings of Goodenough,[27] and in view of the careful method of selection used in both of these studies, the difference can hardly be due to a highly selected group of girls. In fact, girls seem to have higher IQ's in most of the extensive studies in which our standard individual intelligence tests have been used.

Many people who consider that these tests measure what we mean by intelligence interpret this to mean that girls are more intelligent than boys. This may be true if the tests actually measure intelligence, and measure it equally in boys and in girls. In view of the findings of Goodenough,[27] however, it is very doubtful whether or not the tests measure the intelligence of the two sexes equally. She says, "On the first test the girls rank somewhat higher than the boys at all ages, and this apparent superiority is maintained on the second test at ages three and four. The differences are in the same direction and approximately equal to those reported by Terman (*The Measurement of Intelligence*, p. 69)." The figures upon which these statements are based were presented in Chapter II. In another article [26] Goodenough accounts for the sex differences as follows:

It was pointed out before that sex differences on a composite test such as the Binet should not be interpreted as indicating a true difference in the rate of general mental development of the sexes, since such differences may readily result from a selection of items which tends to favor one or the other sex. . . . . Inspection of the separate test items enables us to advance a possible explanation which is at least in accordance with the data presented in an earlier part of this paper. Of the 39 tests from which the scores earned were derived, at least 12 appear to be dependent chiefly upon immediate memory, viz.: repeating digits (three tests), repeating sentences (two tests), picture memory (two tests), reproduction of a series of taps (two tests), memory for three simultaneous commands, recognition of forms, and reproduction of paper folding. . . . . Except for the test of repeating two digits, which shows no consistent sex differences, the girls exceed the boys on all of the tests listed above. A second source of advantage to the girls is to be found in the predominantly verbal character of the greater number of the tests. Certain tests are obviously almost entirely a matter of linguistic ability, ... The girls of our group exceed the boys on all of these tests. . . . . Of the entire group of 39 tests, the boys are consistently superior in only three. . . . . None of these requires a verbal response. Six tests show no consistent sex differences. In these also the verbal element plays a relatively small part. . . . . It has been shown that more than half of the total number of items in the section of the Binet under consideration are chiefly dependent upon types of performance in which females have been found to exceed males at all ages for which information is available, while the types of performance in which males have usually been found to exceed females are practically unrepresented.

We can hardly say that the more precocious linguistic development of the girls is due to a more precocious intellectual development as evidenced by the higher IQ's of the girls, but rather, it is more likely that the higher intelligence test scores obtained by them are due to their more precocious linguistic development. Nice [48] reports a superiority of girls in the extent of vocabulary; Terman [68] reports that the age of the appearance of short sentences in the children of the gifted group was less for the girls than for the boys; Mead [44] found that feeble-minded boys begin to walk and talk later than feeble-minded girls. Doran,[20] on the basis of his elaborate survey of the literature, reports that girls have larger vocabularies than boys of the same age, but that the difference becomes smaller among the older children. He states in conclusion, "We are not warranted in saying which has the better vocabulary after the twenty-fourth month though it is probable that further investigation will show the girls surpass the boys up to the fifth or sixth year." This is in accordance with the report of Magni quoted by Esper,[22] in which the opinion is set forth that boys have smaller vocabularies than girls up to the fifth or sixth year, and that thereafter the boys exceed the girls in the number of words known. It is interesting to note in connection with the findings of the present investigation that Stern [63] says that girls are generally more imitative than boys and pick up words more correctly. Smith,[61] although she found no significant differences in favor of either sex in the number of words to the sentence or in the number of words used in an hour, did find differences in

favor of the girls in her vocabulary test. She says, "Taking, next, the test data and considering particularly the groups in which both the chronological and mental ages are comparable, it seems that, for ages two and three there is a tendency for the girls to be ahead of the boys; but later the boys progress and catch up to the girls."

Thus, from the numerous indications in the literature, as well as from the consistent findings of the present investigation, it appears that girls develop more rapidly in the use of language than do boys at these early ages. Whether or not the difference is maintained at higher ages, we have not sufficient evidence to say, but as indicated above, there seems to be a tendency for the boys to equal or excel the girls in language after the age of five or six years. According to Goodenough,[26] "Paterson and Langlie found that for a selected group of University of Minnesota freshmen, only 36 per cent of the men equalled or exceeded the median score of the women on the Iowa content examination in English, although 61 per cent of the men of this group exceeded the median of the women in the score on the general college ability test." Such findings as these tend to indicate that upon further investigation it may be found that these early tendencies in linguistic ability persist to the adult level.

PATERNAL OCCUPATION AND MENTAL AGE

Throughout the foregoing analyses, differences have been found between the children of the various social classes as they are differentiated by paternal occupation. Chamberlain [12] says that Degerando as early as 1847 "notes that 'the child of the rich understands more words and less actions, and the child of the poor less words and more actions.'" This little notation is interesting from the historical aspect of the problem. The differences noted in the present study are striking, particularly in the length of response and in the complexity

of sentence structure. These differences seem even more significant when we keep the factor of intelligence constant in our tabulations according to mental age, and the differences between the upper and the lower occupational groups still persist. Goodenough [27] points out that occupational class is frequently a differentiating factor in work which has been reported on intelligence testing, not only in the army, but in various school surveys as well. Her study indicates that the differences found for higher ages between occupational classes "are to be found among children of from two to four years of age," and that "however intellectual differences between social classes may originate, they have at least become well established before the age of two years." While it is impossible to draw any definite conclusions, it is possible, as in the case of the sex differences discussed above, that the lower intelligence test scores obtained by the children of the lower occupational groups may be a function of slower linguistic development, and since tests involving linguistic ability preponderate in the standard intelligence tests, the children of the upper occupational groups may also be placed at an advantage in the test situation.

Weight is added to the present findings when we consider those reported by Descoeudres,[16] who used children of the upper and lower classes as they were distinguished by attendance at a private or at a public school. She found that on practically all of the items of her extensive battery of tests, nearly all of which involved language, the children of the upper social classes were decidedly superior to those of the lower social classes.

IMPLICATIONS AND APPLICATIONS

One of the most interesting points brought out by a study such as this, and one which we are likely to lose sight of while we are considering the more detailed results, is the rapid-

ity with which the complex habits involved in learning to speak are acquired by the little child. The age range used in the present investigation is only three years, and yet what a remarkable change we note in the child in that short period. Of course, the preschool period is one of rapid change in all functions, but language is indeed a most rapid acquisition, as it begins late and attains a high degree of perfection at a very early age. The average child of eighteen months is just beginning to use words to communicate his ideas to others. Previously, he could communicate with those around him only by crying and by gestures. By the age of four and one-half years, he is a highly social individual, using language for his every need and desire, not only physical, but intellectual, and in addition he is using all the most complex forms of sentences found in adult conversation, and his vocabulary amounts to several thousand words. A glance at any of the charts in the preceding chapters will suffice to show that the changes that occur are very rapid up to three and one-half years of age. From then on, the developmental process continues at a slower rate for the next few years. The decrease in the percentage of the child's conversation that is incomprehensible (Fig. 6), and the increase in the mean length of response (Fig. 2) are among the most striking changes. This rapid development in such an intricate and distinctly intellectual function is indeed remarkable, when we realize that it occurs in individuals who are decidedly immature physically, and who have mental ages of only two, three, and four years.

In the present investigation, the language of the child has been attacked from a number of aspects. The numbers of children, while inadequate from a statistical point of view, are larger than have been used in previous studies, and have been so selected as to be as representative as possible of the population; and hence, the results more nearly approach normative material than anything that has been available in the literature up to the present time. Descoeudres [16] notes concerning her original study of sixty-five children from two to seven years, the results of which she later confirmed using 300 children, that "il est curieux de voir en considérant le tableau des résultats combien, malgré les différences individuelles énormes, un très petit nombre de sujets suffit à établir de bonnes moyennes pour chaque âge." It has also been found that the method of observation involving the cross-section technique has proved quite satisfactory in this study, and should prove fruitful in further investigations.

The several types of analysis have all measured distinct aspects of linguistic development, and each has proved most interesting and has yielded some suggestive and stimulating results. There are many aspects of child language, however, which have not been considered at all in this study, particularly the factors of pronunciation, of grammatical errors other than omissions, and of speech defects and their correction. All of these aspects are important, not only for the successful social and emotional adjustment of the child, but also from the point of view of pedagogy. It is important first, however, to study the normal development of the function, and such knowledge will aid us in treatment of the abnormal. While little conclusive evidence is presented in the present investigation, it yields many hints and clues for further investigation, which might be worked out by the elaboration of a technique similar to that used in this instance. Such studies should prove of value particularly in the educational field, where the teacher is constantly working with, and training the language mechanisms of the child. The effect of the environment, of the child's associates, of the factor of bilingualism, of the uses to which the child puts his language, of the situations in which language is called forth, are all problems of vital importance and interest not only to psychologists, but to mothers, teachers, and everyone interested in the development of the young child.

CHAPTER VIII

GENERAL SUMMARY

In this investigation an attempt has been made to analyze the development of the language of the child as it occurs in samples of his running conversation. One hundred and forty children were selected in such a way as to give as nearly a random sampling of the preschool population of Minneapolis, Minnesota, as it is practically possible to secure, using paternal occupation as the criterion of selection. The subjects of the experiment ranged from eighteen to fifty-four months of age, and there were twenty at each of seven age levels at six-months intervals. Each age group was discrete, since the children were all examined within a month and a half of the age at which they were classified. Fifty consecutive verbal responses were recorded for each child exactly as they sounded to the experimenter. They were secured during home visits in which the situation was as carefully standardized as it was possible to make home visits to such young children of such different age levels.

Since some of the responses of the youngest children were incomprehensible, they had to be treated separately. The data did not readily lend themselves to the conventional type of grammatical analysis, so these classifications were abandoned. The comprehensible responses were treated according to four types of analysis, all of which proved highly reliable: first, the analysis according to the length of response; second, the analysis according to the function of the response in relation to the child's environment; third, the analysis according to the complexity of sentence structure; and fourth, a word analysis according to the various parts of speech, considering both the total number of words used and the number of different words used.

Each of these analyses was studied in relation to chronological age, sex, mental age, paternal occupation, and to the age of the child's associates. The factor of bilingualism was also considered for the analysis according to the mean length of response.

The analysis according to the length of response yielded the following results:

1. The percentage of comprehensible responses increased rapidly with age, and the girls excelled the boys in this type of response at nearly all ages.

2. The mean length of response shows an increase with chronological age, an increase which is more rapid at the younger age levels.

3. A small but consistent sex difference in favor of the girls for the mean length of response appeared at six of the seven age levels.

4. The mean length of response shows clear differences from one occupational group to the other, each group maintaining its proper relative position very consistently.

5. Trends similar to those shown in relation to chronological age were found for the length of response considered in relation to mental age.

6. Sex differences in the length of response in favor of the girls persist, although they are less marked when mental age is kept constant.

7. Children who associate chiefly with adults show a much greater mean length of response than do those who associate with other children.

8. As indicated by the mean length of response, the hearing of a foreign language in the home does not seem to be a serious handicap in the child's linguistic development.

9. Some indication of initial shyness may be seen in the fact that the first ten responses recorded are shorter on the average than succeeding groups of ten responses.

10. The mean time required to secure fifty responses shows very little change with chronological age or with sex.

The following trends were revealed by the analysis according to the function of the response in relation to the child's environment:

1. The three groups, adapted information, questions, and answers, show marked relative increases with advance in chronological age, while the group of emotionally toned responses shows a relative decrease with advance in chronological age.

2. The categories that show trends with chronological age show them more markedly among the girls than among the boys, indicating a more rapid development of the girls.

3. Analysis of the various subdivisions of the adapted-information category indicates that naming decreases with chronological age, and decreases more rapidly among the girls. Remarks associated with the situation show an increase with chronological age, with a tendency for the girls to be superior.

4. Analysis of the functional categories in relation to paternal occupation reveals a much higher proportion of adapted information and of questions at all ages among the children of the upper occupational groups.

5. No significant trends appear in the analysis according to the age of the child's associates.

6. This functional analysis, when considered in relation to mental age shows the same tendencies, though less markedly, which were indicated in relation to chronological age.

7. With mental age held constant, the differences between the upper and lower occupational groups still persist, although to a less marked degree.

The construction analysis showed several interesting tendencies:

1.   A decrease in the relative proportion of the responses that were functionally complete but structurally incomplete, with a more rapid falling off among the girls.

2.   An initial increase in the proportion of simple sentences, which also occurs first among the girls.

3.   The late appearance of the simple sentence with a phrase, and a marked increase in this group with advance in age, the increase being more rapid among the girls than among the boys.

4.   The compound and complex sentences also appear late and continue as very small proportions throughout the upper age levels.

5.   The elaborated sentence appears in the upper ages and shows a marked increase (which is greater among the girls) with increase in chronological age.

6.   Omission of the verb was the most frequent type of omission, particularly among the younger children. This seems consistent with the predominance of naming noted in the functional analysis and also with the large proportion of nouns found in the vocabularies of the youngest subjects of practically all previous studies.

7.   Omission of the subject was next in importance, appearing as a larger proportion when the precentage of verbs in the vocabulary is increasing.

8.   All of the items of the construction analysis show marked and consistent differences between the upper and the lower occupational groups, which persist, although to a lesser extent, when mental age is held constant.

The word analysis according to the various parts of speech was carried out on two bases: first, according to the total number of words used at each age level, and, second, according to the number of different words used at each age. The first type of analysis seems to indicate the trends with age better than the second. The analysis according to the variety of words used depends, in large measure, on the proportions of the various parts of speech which there are in the language, while that based on the total number of words used gives a better picture of the child's active vocabulary as it is found in samples of running conversation. The following tendencies were indicated in this analysis:

1. Considering the total number of words used, the proportion of nouns in the vocabulary is very large at the younger ages, decreasing with age up to about thirty months.

2. Corresponding to this decrease in the percentage of nouns, there is an increase in the percentage of verbs, with advance in chronological age.

3. The other large increases are to be found in the proportions of adverbs and of pronouns.

4. Conjunctions appear late, as do the prepositions, and both of these categories increase, though slightly, with advance in age.

5. The sex differences are less marked in this analysis than in the foregoing analyses, and though the same tendencies appear with advance in mental age as appeared with increase in chronological age, the sex differences disappear when we hold mental age constant.

6. When the parts of speech analysis based on the total number of words used were studied in relation to paternal occupation, the results failed to confirm the theory of Drever,[21] who maintains that the children with broader environments tend to have relatively more nouns and fewer verbs than the children of more narrow experience.

As has been pointed out, most of the previous investigations in the field of the language development of the young child have been done under poorly controlled conditions.   In this study every precaution has been taken to secure carefully controlled experimentation.   Since this study is of a normative nature, the selection of the subjects is of vital importance. The number of subjects used is larger than in most of the previous studies, and the best method that we now know of securing a representative group has been very carefully followed.   This investigation has further contributed to methodology by the use of the cross-section method with short, controlled observations on a large number of children.   This type of approach has proved very profitable and is a practical method to use in studying such functions in young children. The various types of analysis employed proved highly reliable and should be fruitful in further work.   The results bring out clear-cut differences, indicating a more rapid development of language among girls, and they also show earlier language development among the children of the upper socio-economic classes.   Perhaps the most striking result of all, however, is the remarkable speed with which this whole developmental process occurs.   The child at eighteen months of age knows only a few single words, and yet in a short time—three years— he has acquired several thousand words, which he is able to combine into sentences as long and as complex as the adult uses in his everyday conversation; he has a ready command of all the inflections of the language and can use language for communicating all his thoughts, needs, and desires.

APPENDIX

APPENDIX

In this appendix are presented three sample records of the responses of children two, three, and four years of age. They were selected because the score for the length of response for these children was nearest to the mean length for each age level represented. The responses are presented together with the scoring of each response according to the various types of analysis. Words or sentences in parentheses were said by the experimenter, or by the mother, and directly influenced the child's response.

L. T.—GIRL, AGE 24 MONTHS. OCCUPATIONAL GROUP V.
TIME, 13 MINUTES.

No.	Response	Function	Construction	Length Words	Syl.
	(Would you like to look at this picture-book?)				
1.	All right.	Answer	Func. Complete	2	
	(What do you see in that picture?)				
2.	A baby.	Answer	Func. Complete	2	
3.	Da doggie.	Naming	Verb Omitted	2	
4.	Da doggie.	Naming	Verb Omitted	2	
5.	Da doggie.	Naming	Verb Omitted	2	
6.	Da boy.	Naming	Verb Omitted	2	
	(What has the little boy?)				
7.	A dollie.	Answer	Func. Complete	2	
8.	What's that, what's that?	Question	Simple Sent.	6	
9.	Dere's one!	Immed. Sit.	Simple Sent.	3	
10.	Dere's one!	Immed. Sit.	Simple Sent.	3	
11.	What's there?	Question	Simple Sent.	3	
12.	There.	Immed. Sit.	Func. Complete	1	
13.	That one de we dat.	Semicompre.	....		5
14.	Dere's one oo.	Immed. Sit.	Simple Sent.	4	
15.	Dere one da mite.	Semicompre.	....		4
16.	Der.	Immed. Sit.	Func. Complete	1	
17.	De de.	Rep. of Sound	....		2
18.	Da.	Single Sound	....		1
19.	Da boy.	Naming	Verb Omitted	2	

159

No.	Response	Function	Construction	Length Words	Syl.
20.	Doggie.	Naming	Func. Complete	1	
21.	Da kitty. (What has the kitty?)	Naming	Verb Omitted	2	
22.	Da tail. (Yes, and what else?)	Answer	Func. Complete	2	
23.	Eyes.	Answer	Func. Complete	1	
24.	Ian. (What do you think this is?)	Varied sounds	....		2
25.	Telephone.	Answer	Func. Complete	1	
26.	Doggie.	Naming	Func. Complete	1	
27.	Boy.	Naming	Func. Complete	1	
28.	Ah de way den.	Varied Sounds	....		4
29.	Telephone don' go.	Criticism	Simple Sent.	3	
30.	Det dat.	Emotional	Simple Sent.	2	
31.	I wan see. (What do you think this is?)	Emotional	Prep. Omitted	3	
32.	Dat ka book. (What does the kitty say?)	Answer	....		3
33.	Say ee ee.	Answer	Subj. Omitted	2	
34.	Kitty.	Naming	Func. Complete	1	
35.	Da horsie. (Where is the horsie?)	Naming	Verb Omitted	2	
36.	Right there.	Answer	Func. Complete	2	
37.	Ea doggie bum. (Are you going to call up your daddy?)	Semicompre.	....		4
38.	No, I gonna call up mamma.	Answer	Verb Omitted	7	
39.	I call up Dace.	Assoc. w. Sit.	Verb Omitted	4	
40.	An de be da. (Whom do you see in this picture?)	Varied Sounds	....		4
41.	Jimmie.	Answer	Func. Complete	1	
42.	Da mouth.	Naming	Verb Omitted	2	

No.	Response	Function	Construction	Length Words	Syl.
43.	Right there.	Immed. Sit.	Func. Complete	2	
44.	Street car.	Naming	Func. Complete	1	
45.	Street car. (What color is the car?)	Repetition	Func. Complete	1	
46.	Red.	Answer	Func. Complete	1	
47.	Hello.	Soc. Phrase	Func. Complete	1	
48.	Hello.	Soc. Phrase	Func. Complete	1	
49.	Dat mine.	Immed. Sit.	Verb Omitted	2	
50.	An a det a dat.	Varied Sounds	....		5

J. Z.—BOY, AGE 36 MONTHS. OCCUPATIONAL GROUP IV. TIME, 15 MINUTES.

No.	Response	Function	Construction	Length Words	Syl.
	(What do you see in that picture?)				
1.	Them cows.	Answer	Func. Complete	2	
2.	Them horses in there.	Naming	Verb Omitted	4	
3.	I seen pigs over to grandpa's house.	Assoc. w. Sit.	Simple w. Phrase	7	
4.	Pigs.	Naming	Func. Complete	1	
5.	Da cow no.	Immed. Sit.	Verb Omitted	3	
6.	Two cows.	Immed. Sit.	Func. Complete	2	
7.	Da cow.	Naming	Func. Complete	2	
8.	Horsa.	Naming	Func. Complete	1	
9.	De cows dat is.	Naming	Simple Sent.	4	
10.	Got a top on here.	Immed. Sit.	Subj. Omitted	5	
11.	Got a wheel on here, ain't we?	Immed. Sit.	Subj. Omitted	7	
12.	Here comes a cow?	Question	Simple Sent.	5	
13.	What's dat?	Question	Simple Sent.	3	
14.	What's dat?	Question	Simple Sent.	3	
15.	Zat come cow on.	Semicompre.	....		4
16.	Dem cows.	Naming	Verb Omitted	2	
17.	This is a catty.	Naming	Simple Sent.	4	

No.	Response	Function	Construction	Length Words Syl.
18.	Like dat cow.	Immed. Sit.	Subj. Omitted	3
19.	He grandpa bring cows.	Assoc. w. Sit.	Simple Sent.	4
20.	Here comes the kitty—big kitty.	Immed. Sit.	Simple Sent.	6
21.	What is dat?	Question	Simple Sent.	3
22.	What is dat?	Question	Simple Sent.	3
23.	Dat's a catty.	Naming	Simple Sent.	4
24.	Here's a catty.	Naming	Simple Sent.	4
25.	What is that?	Question	Simple Sent.	3
26.	What is that?	Question	Simple Sent.	3
27.	Like de cows.	Immed. Sit.	Subj. Omitted	3
28.	I like de little car.	Immed. Sit.	Simple Sent.	5
29.	Dat my little car.	Immed. Sit.	Verb Omitted	4
30.	Fix de car.	Emotional	Simple Sent.	3
31.	My daddy fix our car.	Assoc. w. Sit.	Simple Sent.	5
32.	I broke a choo-choo train.	Assoc. w. Sit.	Simple Sent.	4
33.	I took it out and it fall off.	Assoc. w. Sit.	Compound Sent.	8
34.	It fell off my hands.	Assoc. w. Sit.	Simp. w. Phrase	5
35.	Car.	Naming	Func. Complete	1
36.	What is dat?	Question	Simple Sent.	3
37.	Where's cows?	Question	Simple Sent.	3
38.	What is this?	Question	Simple Sent.	3
39.	Dat wa like da cows da.	Immed. Sit.	Simp. w. Phrase	6
40.	Cat.	Naming	Func. Complete	1
41.	Make on a dogs.	Assoc. w. Sit.	Subj. Omitted	4
42.	Dogs get cow.	Assoc. w. Sit.	Simple Sent.	3
43.	Run on da cows.	Assoc. w. Sit.	Subj. Omitted	4
44.	Run on da cows.	Repetition	Subj. Omitted	4
45.	Run on da pigs.	Repetition	Subj. Omitted	4
46.	Whose is it?	Question	Simple Sent.	3
47.	Wha is dere?	Question	Simple Sent.	3
48.	What is dis?	Question	Simple Sent.	3
49.	A baby.	Naming	Func. Complete	2
50.	What is dis?	Question	Simple Sent.	3

M. M.—Girl, Age 48 Months. Occupational Group II.
Time, 15 Minutes.

No.	Response	Function	Construction	Length Words	Syl.
1.	Goosie Gander.	Naming	Func. Complete	1	
2.	Did ya give my cousin that? (Who is your cousin?)	Question	Simp.Sent.w.Phrase	6	
3.	She plays with me.	Answer	Simp.Sent.w.Phrase	4	
4.	Sometimes she bees naughty.	Assoc. w. Sit.	Simple Sent.	4	
5.	Do you know what we got?	Question	Complex Sent.	6	
6.	A bicycle. (What do you do with it?)	Assoc. w. Sit.	Func. Complete	2	
7.	Ride it down the hill. (In front of your house?)	Answer	Func. Complete	5	
8.	Sure, right out here.	Answer	Func. Complete	4	
9.	I know what that book's about.	Immed. Sit.	Complex	7	
10.	Is that a boy?	Question	Simple Sent.	4	
11.	Look at the big tassel-cap.	Immed. Sit.	Simp.Sent.w.Phrase	5	
12.	What's this about? (What do you think?)	Question	Simp.Sent.w.Phrase	4	
13.	A sheep.	Answer	Func. Complete	2	
14.	I know this one.	Immed. Sit.	Simple Sent.	4	
15.	Shall I turn another page?	Question	Simple Sent.	5	
16.	What's this about?	Question	Simp.Sent.w.Phrase	4	
17.	What's this?	Question	Simple Sent.	3	
18.	How big is it?	Question	Simple Sent.	4	
19.	What's this?	Question	Simple Sent.	3	
20.	I read him.	Immed. Sit.	Simple Sent.	3	
21.	Is this all water?	Question	Simple Sent.	4	
22.	What's this little girl doing?	Question	Simple Sent.	6	

No.	Response	Function	Construction	Length Words Syl.
23.	What's this little boy doing?	Question	Simple Sent.	6
24.	Is he fishing?	Question	Simple Sent.	3
25.	Where is the other bird going?	Question	Simple Sent.	6
26.	What are these?	Question	Simple Sent.	3
27.	What are all these?	Question	Simple Sent.	4
28.	Can I read another book?	Question	Simple Sent.	5
29.	What's this?	Question	Simple Sent.	3
30.	What are they eating?	Question	Simple Sent.	4
31.	What's this?	Question	Simple Sent.	3
32.	What's this here?	Question	Simple Sent.	4
33.	All these are foxes here too, aren't they?	Question	Simple Sent.	8
34.	Here's a kitty.	Naming	Simple Sent.	4
35.	What's this? Cow?	Question	Simple Sent.	4
36.	Here a horse.	Naming	Verb Omitted	3
37.	What's the pig doing?	Question	Simple Sent.	5
38.	Here's something.	Immed. Sit.	Simple Sent.	3
39.	What's that?	Question	Simple Sent.	3
40.	What's this here?	Question	Simple Sent.	4
41.	Can he stand?	Question	Simple Sent.	3
42.	Can I put him on the floor?	Question	Simp.Sent.w.Phrase	7
43.	He's walking to my mamma.	Immed. Sit.	Simp.Sent.w.Phrase	6
44.	Walk kitty.	Emotional	Simple Sent.	2
45.	Walk to my mamma.	Emotional	Simp.Sent.w.Phrase	4
46.	You have to catch him.	Emotional	Simp.Sent.w.Phrase	5
47.	He's coming back to you.	Immed. Sit.	Simp.Sent.w.Phrase	6
48.	Lookit, he fell. (Can the kitty talk?)	Immed. Sit.	Simple Sent.	3
49.	He can't.	Answer	Simple Sent.	2
50.	You make him.	Emotional	Simple Sent.	3

BIBLIOGRAPHY

1. ALLPORT, F. H. *Social Psychology.* New York: Houghton Mifflin Co. 1924.
2. BATEMAN, W. G. "A Child's Progress in Speech." *Journal of Educational Psychology,* 5: 307-320. 1914.
3. ————. "The Language Status of Three Children at the Same Ages." *Pedagogical Seminary,* 23: 211-240. 1916.
4. ————. "Papers on Language Development. I. The First Word." *Pedagogical Seminary,* 24: 391-398. 1917.
5. ————. "Two Children's Progress in Speech." *Journal of Educational Psychology,* 6: 475-493. 1915.
6. BEYER, T. P. "Vocabulary of Two Years." *Educational Review,* 50: 191-203. 1915.
7. BOYD, WM. "The Development of a Child's Vocabulary." *Pedagogical Seminary,* 21: 95-124. 1914.
8. BRANDENBURG, G. C. "The Language of a Three-Year-Old Child." *Pedagogical Seminary,* 22: 89-120. 1915.
9. BRANDENBURG, G. C., and BRANDENBURG, J. "Language Development during the Fourth Year." *Pedagogical Seminary,* 23: 14-29. 1916.
10. ————. "Language Development during the Fourth Year: The Conversation." *Pedagogical Seminary,* 26: 27-40. 1919.
11. CARR, HARVEY. *Psychology,* Chap. VIII. New York: Longmans, Green & Co. 1925.
12. CHAMBERLAIN, A. F. *The Child: A Study in the Evolution of Man,* Chap. V, 495. London: W. Scott, Ltd. 1903.
13. CHAMPNEYS, F. H. "Notes on an Infant." *Mind,* 6: 104-107. 1881.
14. CONRADI, E. "The Psychology and Pathology of Speech Development." *Pedagogical Seminary,* 11: 328-380. 1904.
15. DARWIN, CHARLES. "Biographical Sketch of an Infant." *Mind,* 2: 285-294. 1877.
16. DESCOEUDRES, ALICE. *Le développement de l'enfant de deux à sept ans.* Paris: Delachaux & Niéstle. 1921.
17. DEVILLE, G. "Notes sur le Développement du Langue." *Revue Linguistique et Philologique Comparatif,* 23: 330-343. 1890.
18. DEWEY, JOHN. *How We Think.* Boston: D. C. Heath & Co. 1910.
19. ————. "The Psychology of Infant Language." *Psychological Review,* 1: 63-66. 1894.

20. DORAN, E. W. "A Study of Vocabularies." *Pedagogical Seminary*, 14: 401-438. 1907.

21. DREVER, J. "A Study of Children's Vocabularies, I, II, and III." *Journal of Experimental Pedagogy*, 3:34-43, 96-103, 182-188. 1915-1916.

22. ESPER, ERWIN A. "Psychology of Language." *Psychological Bulletin*, 18: 490-496. 1921.

23. GALE, H. "The Vocabularies of Three Children in One Family at Two and Three Years of Age." *Pedagogical Seminary*, 9: 422-433. 1902.

24. GALE, M. C., and GALE, H. "Children's Vocabularies." *Popular Science Monthly*, 61: 45-51. 1901.

25. ————. "Vocabularies of Three Children of One Family to Two-and-One-Half Years of Age." *Psychological Studies*, No. 1, pp. 70-117. 1906.

26. GOODENOUGH, FLORENCE L. "Consistency of Sex Differences in Mental Traits at Various Ages." *Psychological Review*, 34: 440-462. 1927.

27. ————. *The Kuhlman-Binet Tests. A Critical Study and Evaluation*, Institute of Child Welfare, University of Minnesota Monograph Series No. II. Minneapolis: The University of Minnesota Press. 1928.

28. GRANT, J. R. "A Child's Vocabulary and Its Growth." *Pedagogical Seminary*, 22: 183-203. 1915.

29. GUILLAUME, P. "Le développement des elements formels dans le language de l'enfant." *Journal de Psychologie*, 24:203-229. 1927.

30. HALL, G. S. "Notes on the Study of Infants." *Pedagogical Seminary*, 1: 127-238. 1891.

31. HINCKLEY, ALICE C. "A Case of Retarded Speech Development." *Pedagogical Seminary*, 22: 121-146. 1915.

32. HULL, CLARK L., and QUITZI, BERTHA. "Parallel Learning Curves of an Infant in Vocabulary and Control of the Bladder." *Pedagogical Seminary*, 26: 272-283. 1919.

33. JESPERSON, O. *Language, Its Nature, Development and Origin*. London: Allen & Winous Co. 1922.

34. KELLER, HELEN. *The Story of My Life*. Garden City: Doubleday, Page & Co. 1922.

35. KIRKPATRICK, E. A. *Fundamentals of Child Study*. New York: The Macmillan Co. 1903.

36. ———— "The Number of Words in Ordinary Vocabularies." *Science*, 18: 107-108. 1891.

37. KOFFKA, K. *The Growth of the Mind.* New York: Harcourt, Brace & Co. 1924.

38. LUKENS, H. "Preliminary Report on the Learning of Language." *Pedagogical Seminary*, 3: 424-460. 1894.

39. MACDOUGALL, ROBERT. "The Child's Speech." *Journal of Educational Psychology*, 3: 423-429, 507-513 (1912) ; 4: 29-38. 1913.

40. MAGNI, JOHN A. "Vocabularies." *Pedagogical Seminary*, 26: 207-233. 1919.

41. MAJOR, D. R. *First Steps in Mental Growth.* New York: The Macmillan Co. 1906.

42. MARSTON, L. R. *The Emotions of Young Children—A Study in Introversion and Extroversion*, University of Iowa Studies in Child Welfare, III, No. 3. 1925.

43. MEAD, C. D. *The Relation of General Intelligence to Certain Mental and Physical Traits*, Bureau of Publications, Teachers College, Columbia University. 1916.

44. ————. "The Age of Walking and Talking in Relation to General Intelligence." *Pedagogical Seminary*, 20: 460-484. 1913.

45. MEUMANN, E. *Die Entstehung der ersten Wortbedeutungen beim Kinde.* Leipzig: W. Engelmann. 1902.

46. MOORE, K. C. "The Mental Development of a Child." *Psychological Review Monograph*, Supplement 1, No. 3, pp. 1-145. 1896.

47. MURCHISON, CARL, and LANGER, SUZANNE. "Tiedemann's Observations on the Development of the Mental Faculties of Children." *Pedagogical Seminary and Journal of Genetic Psychology*, 34: 205-230. 1927.

48. NICE, M. M. "Ambidexterity and Delayed Speech Development." *Pedagogical Seminary*, 25: 141-162. 1918.

49. ————. "Concerning All-Day Conversations." *Pedagogical Seminary*, 27: 166-177. 1920.

50. ————. "Length of Sentences as a Criterion of a Child's Progress in Speech." *Journal of Educational Psychology*, 16: 370-379. 1925.

51. ————. "Speech Development of a Child from Eighteen Months to Six Years." *Pedagogical Seminary*, 24: 204-243. 1917.

52. Noire, Ludwig. *The Origin and Philosophy of Language.* Chicago: Open Court Publishing Co. 1917.

53. O'Shea, M. V. *Linguistic Development and Education.* New York: The Macmillan Co. 1907.

54. Pelsma, John R. "A Child's Vocabulary and Its Development." *Pedagogical Seminary,* 17: 328-369. 1910.

55. Perez, B. *The First Three Years of Childhood.* 2nd ed. Syracuse: C. W. Bardeen. 1899.

56. Piaget, Jean. *The Language and Thought of the Child.* New York: Harcourt, Brace & Co. 1926.

57. Pollock, F. "An Infant's Progress in Language." *Mind,* 3: 392-401. 1878.

58. Preyer, Wm. *Mental Development in the Child.* Trans. from the German by H. W. Brown. International Educational Series. New York: D. Appleton & Co. 1901.

59. —————. *The Development of the Intellect.* Part II, "The Mind of the Child." New York: D. Appleton & Co. 1889.

60. Robinson, E. S., and Robinson, F. R. *Readings in General Psychology.* Chicago: University of Chicago Press. 1923.

61. Smith, Madorah E. *An Investigation of the Development of the Sentence and the Extent of Vocabulary in Young Children,* University of Iowa Studies in Child Welfare, III, No. 5. 1926.

62. Snyder, Alice D. "Notes on the Talk of a Two-and-One-Half Year Old Boy." *Pedagogical Seminary,* 21: 412-424. 1914.

63. Stern, Wm. *Psychology of Early Childhood,* Part III. New York: Henry Holt & Co. 1924.

64. Sully, James. *Studies of Childhood.* New York: D. Appleton & Co. 1896.

65. Symposium. "Is Thinking Merely the Action of Language Mechanisms?" *British Journal of Psychology,* 11: 55-104. 1920.

66. Taine, H. "Acquisition of Language by Children." *Mind,* 2: 252-259. 1877.

67. Tanner, A. E. *The Child, His Thinking, Feeling, and Doing.* Chicago: Rand, McNally & Co. 1903.

68. Terman, L. M. *Genetic Studies of Genius,* Vol. I. Stanford University Press, Stanford University. 1926.

69. Thorson, Agnes M. "The Relation of Tongue Movements to Internal Speech." *Journal of Experimental Psychology,* 8: 1-32. 1925.

for

70. TITCHENER, E. B. *A Primer of Psychology.* New York: The Macmillan Co. 1899.
71. WATSON, J. B. *Behaviorism.* New York: People's Institute Publishing Co. 1925.
72. ————. *Behavior—An Introduction to Comparative Psychology.* New York: Henry Holt & Co. 1914.
73. ————. *Psychology from the Standpoint of a Behaviorist,* Chap. IX. Philadelphia: J. B. Lippincott Co. 1924.
74. ————. "The Unverbalized in Human Behavior." *Psychological Review,* 31: 273-280. 1924.
75. WHIPPLE, G. M., and WHIPPLE, MRS. G. M. "The Vocabulary of a Three-Year-Old Boy, with Some Interpretive Comments." *Pedagogical Seminary,* 15:1-22. 1909.
76. WUNDT, WM. *Outlines of Psychology.* Trans. by C. H. Judd. 3rd ed. Leipzig: G. E. Stechert. 1907.
77. WYCZOIKOWSKA, ANNA. "Theoretical and Experimental Studies in the Mechanism of Speech." *Psychological Review,* 20: 448-458. 1913.
78. YERKES, R. M., and LEARNED, B. W. *Chimpanzee's Intelligence and Its Vocal Expression.* Baltimore: Williams & Wilkins Co. 1925.
79. ZYVE, C. I. "Conversation among Children." *Teachers College Record,* 29: 46-61. 1927.

INDEX

Adapted information, 39-40, 78, 87-88, 91-92, 153; analysis of, 83 ff.; sex differences in, 82

Adjectives, 15, 18-19, 21, 94, 112, 115, 117

Adverbs, 19-20, 22, 94, 113, 117, 155

Age, chronological, and construction analysis, 96 ff.; and functional analysis, 71 ff.; and length of response, 53 ff.; and word analysis, 113 ff.; distribution by, 27; of subjects, 24 ff.

Age of associates, 35, 92, 106, 150; and construction analysis, 106, 153; and functional analysis, 71 ff., 88, 153; and length of response, 62 ff., 69, 152; and mental age in construction analysis, 109; and mental age in functional analysis, 91

Age, mental, 22-23; and construction analysis, 106 ff., 110, 154; and functional analysis, 88 ff., 92, 153; and length of response, 58 ff., 152; and paternal occupation, 61 ff., 90 ff., 109, 147 ff.; and sex differences, 144 ff.; and word analysis, 120 ff., 155; sources of error, 58 ff. *See also* Age of Associates, construction analysis

Allport, F. H., 5, 137

Ament, W., 7, 132

Analysis of data, methods of, 35 ff.; results of, Chaps. III, IV, V, VI

Answers, 39, 41, 81, 91, 153

Articles, 13, 21-22, 44, 93, 112

Articulation, 23, 33

Auxiliaries, 13, 93-94, 113

Babbling, 6 ff., 36, 94

Barr, Taussig classification, 26

Bartlett, F. C., and Smith, E. M., 140

Bateman, W. G., 4, 10, 14-15, 132; rules, 45 ff.

Beyer, T. P., 15

Bilingualism, 65 ff., 69, 150, 152

Binet, Alfred, 145-146

"Bow-wow" theory, 128

Boyd, William, 15, 19, 54

Brandenburgs, the, 4, 14, 16

Carr, Harvey, 141

Chamberlain, A. F., 4, 130, 147

Champneys, F. H., 8

Claparède, E., 38, 70

Clauses, 44, 101

Condillac, E. B. de, 133

Conjunctions, 13, 20, 22, 44, 116, 119, 155

Conradi, E., 8

Consonants, appearance of, 6 ff.

Construction analysis, method of, 42 ff. *See also* Age of Associates, Age, Paternal occupation, Reliability, Response, Sex

Contraction, of subject and predicate, 36; of verb and negative, 36

Conversation, all day, 14; parts of speech in, 20 ff.

Criticism, 39, 41, 78

Cross-section method, 125, 127, 144, 156

Darwin, Charles, 8, 130

Data, collection of, 24 ff. *See also* Analysis of data

Degerando, M., 147

Descoeudres, Alice, 22, 148, 150

Developmental stages, 6 ff.

Deville, G., 15

Dewey, John, 18, 37, 139

Dissyllables, 10

Doran, E. W., 14, 55, 60, 146

Dramatic imitation, 39, 42, 81

Drever, J., 16, 19-20, 123